"Kris sounds a clear prophetic call to embrace change. Throughout the pages of this book he commissions us to make earth like heaven. You will receive an impartation of supernatural faith and courage as you journey through the pages of this book and become part of the Kingdom mandate to transform society."

Ché Ahn, apostle, Harvest Apostolic Center;
apostolic leader, HRock Church

"Kris charges ahead with the spirit of Caleb and Joshua to say that God has given us the greatest opportunity ever to bring in His Kingdom with power and love, integrity and victory. *Heavy Rain* will motivate new Christians, students and old saints alike to shake off that which hinders, and run for God. I learned so much; I am reading this book again."

John Arnott, Catch the Fire Toronto

"Our very good friend Kris Vallotton has written a positive, detailed vision of the church as an effective catalyst for world transformation through the demonstration of both power and love. He and his church have transformed our own family and ministry by genuine apostolic love and friendship, and we are so encouraged by this. Thought-provoking, and controversial in places, he makes a strong case for the Church to set out to improve the world rather than let the devil steal our future. This is our present mandate as Christians and leaders, even as we look forward to the last days, when God will glorify Himself and bring back His Son in magnificent power and majesty."

Rolland and Heidi Baker, founding directors, Iris Global

"Kris Vallotton lives what he writes. He is the revolutionary who puts fire in my bones. He is gifted to understand human relationships and the dynamics that trigger revival. I am glad he is on our side. In this book he explains revelatory truth, but more importantly, he imparts fire. Don't just read this. Catch it!"

Harold R. Eberle, founder, Worldcast Ministries

"*Heavy Rain* is a perspective of the spiritual world we live in that is like seeing from Google Earth. It will draw the reader into Kris's core messages of the last couple of years. He does a masterful job assembling a collage of snapshots that build a highway of revelation to what the Spirit is doing in this coming apostolic age. True to form, Kris will challenge you to think outside the lines as he introduces numerous new dynamics that are in play in this generation. Read this book with an expectation of transformation."

Danny Silk, senior leadership team, Bethel Church, Redding, California, and Jesus Culture, Sacramento, California; founder, Loving on Purpose; author, *Developing a Culture of Honor* and *Loving Our Kids on Purpose*

"No one can read a work out of Bethel Church, Redding, California, without the awareness of the culture and atmosphere in which it was produced. I was recently privileged with the opportunity of spending a week around Bethel, its leaders, its people, its students and servants, where the culture of honor is well-known. You would be interested to know that my report is that it is real and universally atmospheric.

"To know Kris Vallotton is to be acquainted with honor and to see and sense this atmosphere. Hard-hitting, direct and prophetic, but oh so gentle, the author of this book lives what he writes. If one is offended by what is written within these pages, it is probably in part because of the lack of acquaintance with Kris himself. Another consideration for offense is dealing with entrenched traditions that are being hammered herein.

"Honor is inseparable from favor, respect and acceptance. When one chooses honor, as has the whole Bethel team, these qualities are inevitable and real.

"Yes, you will be challenged, shocked, and, if open-minded, you will be beneficially stretched. Reading *Heavy Rain* likely will be similar to being in a pouring rain, a cold-water-in-your-face experience coupled with a blurred view of one's surroundings. But when the rain is over and the view clears, you will be different!"

Jack Taylor, president, Dimensions Ministries, Melbourne, Florida

"The Church as most Americans think of it may help some individuals, but it cannot be a viable means to reform our society. Why? *Heavy Rain* is the most insightful book I have yet encountered that answers that question. The creative suggestions that Kris Vallotton makes for correcting our past weaknesses and reforming our churches are powerful, positive and productive. I want to be part of the exciting kind of Church that I read about here, and I believe you will agree!"

C. Peter Wagner, founder and chancellor emeritus, Wagner Leadership Institute

HEAVY
RAIN

Other Books and Messages by Kris Vallotton

BOOKS

Developing a Supernatural Lifestyle

The Supernatural Ways of Royalty

Basic Training for the Supernatural Ways of Royalty

Basic Training for the Prophetic Ministry

Moral Revolution

Spirit Wars

School of the Prophets

Fashioned to Reign

Outrageous Courage

Supernatural Power of Forgiveness

MESSAGES

Casting Vision, Catching Hearts

Developing a Legacy

Is Your House Haunted?

Fighting for Your Place in History

For the Love of God

From Paupers to Princes

Fear Is Not Your Friend

From the Pool to the River

Mercy Triumphs over Judgment

Leadership for an Epoch Season 1, 2 & 3

The Tipping Point

Living from Eternity

These and many other titles are available at

www.kvministries.com

REVISED AND UPDATED EDITION

HEAVY RAIN

HOW TO FLOOD YOUR WORLD
WITH GOD'S TRANSFORMING POWER

KRIS VALLOTTON

Chosen

a division of Baker Publishing Group
Minneapolis, Minnesota

Published by Chosen Books
11400 Hampshire Avenue South
Bloomington, Minnesota 55438
www.chosenbooks.com

Chosen Books is a division of
Baker Publishing Group, Grand Rapids, Michigan

Previous edition published by Regal Books as *How Heaven Invades Earth*

Printed in the United States of America

Library of Congress Control Number: 2016931539

ISBN 978-0-8007-9782-9

Unless otherwise indicated, Scripture quotations are from the New American Standard Bible®, copyright © 1960, 1962, 1963, 1968, 1971, 1972, 1973, 1975, 1977, 1995 by The Lockman Foundation. Used by permission. (www.Lockman.org)

Scripture quotations identified MESSAGE are from THE MESSAGE. Copyright © by Eugene H. Peterson 1993, 1994, 1995, 1996, 2000, 2001, 2002. Used by permission of NavPress. All rights reserved. Represented by Tyndale House Publishers, Inc.

Scripture quotations identified NKJV are from the New King James Version®. Copyright © 1982 by Thomas Nelson, Inc. Used by permission. All rights reserved.

Scripture quotations identified KJV are from the King James Version of the Bible.

Cover design by LOOK Design Studio

16   17   18   19   20   21   22   7   6   5   4   3   2   1

"And it shall be in the last days," God says, "that I will pour forth of My Spirit on all mankind."

Acts 2:17

I dedicate this book to my children's children's children's children. Though we will not meet until we get to heaven, I wanted you to know that I had you in mind as I wrote every word of this book, and I continue to hold you in my heart. You will become the answer to my prayers and the fulfillment of my prophecies. By the time you read this book, I will be watching you from heaven (see Hebrews 12:1).

Contents

CONTENTS

Foreword

The disciples expected Jesus to establish His earthly Kingdom at any moment. They were counting on Him to take Israel back to the rightful place of influence it once had under Kings David and Solomon. Cities and nations would then live in the fulfillment of a much-anticipated promise under the glorious reign of their Messiah. This thought captured so much of the disciples' attention that they were vying for top honors in His Kingdom. There was a flaw in their thinking, and therefore in their expectations, so Jesus told them a story—a parable (see Luke 19:11–17).

He told them about a landowner who gave a mina (a sum of money) to each of his ten servants. They were to invest that money and make a profit for their master so that upon his return he could gather his earnings. When the first servant came to him, he reported that the master's mina had earned him ten more minas. Then the landowner did something very unusual. He told the servant he was now in charge of ten cities. In one moment the faithful servant became a ruler.

This parable answered at least two of the issues the disciples had not seen clearly. The first was that they were looking for a *sudden event* to make Jesus ruler of cities and nations, but Jesus took them to the *process* of stewardship. Simply speaking, He taught them that correctly stewarding what God puts in our hands increases our influence over humanity—specifically cities. Second, it reveals how we get personal promotion: through faithfulness in whatever God assigns to us. Going from a servant to a governor is quite a promotion. And when that promotion brings the influence of the King of kings through that servant to a whole city, we see a practical manifestation of the Kingdom on earth.

This story reveals how simple the subject of the Kingdom can be. And that is the message of *Heavy Rain*. My dear friend and author Kris Vallotton has done a great job capturing the heart of God for the Church in these last days. You will not find any charts, predictions about the Antichrist, discussions on the tribulation or any of the other hot-button subjects. Instead, this is a book about heart, God's heart. And that discovery is what shapes our attitude, focus and priorities more than any other. That is what excites me about this book: Kris puts his attention on where we have responsibility, not where we have curiosity. His insights are consistent with the theme of the Gospel that "whatever is not from faith is sin." We must be wary of any teaching of the last days that does not require faith to obtain what God promises.

We live at a time when it seems the evil of this world is becoming more pronounced, while the glory of God in the Church is also being put on display in more glorious and obvious manners. Dick Joyce, a prophet and dear friend of both Kris and me, once shared a prophetic word with us that went something like this: "Just as a jeweler lays a piece of black velvet across the counter upon which to display his precious gems, so the Lord is using the darkness of world circumstances as the backdrop for His display of His glory in the church." For me, this word helps settle the tension we face anytime we discuss the subject of the last days—darkness and light, both increasing.

We must learn to be people of great hope, regardless of world circumstances. Jesus always has a victorious plan in place. It is up to us to discover and implement that plan. *Heavy Rain* is sure to play a significant role in releasing the people of God into their glorious role in these glorious days.

Bill Johnson, senior leader, Bethel Church, Redding, California; bestselling author, *When Heaven Invades Earth* and *The Power That Changes the World*

Acknowledgments

Kathy: You are the woman of my dreams and my best friend. Thank you for believing in me when I failed so miserably and reminding me of who I am in God.

Mom: Thanks for loving me and supporting me my entire life.

Grandpa: You taught me how to be a man and loved me when my father died when I was three years old. Although you have gone on to be with the Lord, your life still lives on through me.

Jaime and Marty: I love you both so much. I am very proud that you are part of my legacy. Your encouragement in my life has been invaluable. You are both world-class leaders.

Shannon and Cameron: I love you. You inspire me to believe God for the people whom others throw away. You have done such an amazing job of pastoring Mountain Chapel, the place where this movement all started.

Jason: I love your wisdom in my life. Your insight into the Kingdom is nothing less than supernatural. Your strength has often encouraged me to press on in hard times. I love you, son.

Gene: You inspire all of us with your life. Your ability to overcome impossible obstacles gives me courage to touch others with God's love. I am proud of you, son.

Bill and Beni: Serving God with you has been a dream come true. Your example in my life and in the Body of Christ gave me the inspiration to write this book.

Bill Derryberry: Your life is an inspiration to me. Your love has brought me wholeness.

Danny, Dann, Charlie and Paul: You have helped to shape my life, my ideas and my destiny. I love you with my whole heart.

Bethel team: Wow! You are amazing! It is a privilege to serve with you all.

Introduction

THE REASON

I originally published this book in 2010, and I felt as though it was the best book I had ever written. In fact, I believed *Heavy Rain* could revolutionize the Church as we know it. But the book turned out to be somewhat anachronistic—belonging to or appropriate to a period other than that in which it existed—and it only sold about sixty thousand copies.

Recently, I began to reread the original manuscript and contemplate how much the world has changed in just five short years. In that process, I began to feel as though *Heavy Rain* is actually much more relevant to today's global climate than it was to the time in which I wrote it five years ago. That was the initial reason that I began to look at writing this revised edition.

Yet I also realized that I desperately needed to update the book for three other reasons. First, I have learned a lot more about cultural transformation by working in our own city in the last five years with quite a bit of success. Second, the ISIS-ISIL crisis has escalated to a point where radical Muslims are dramatically affecting the culture of the globe. In my original manuscript, I did not really address the ISIS-ISIL brand of brutal terrorism, nor did I look at the subsequent side effects to both the people who are fleeing and to those who are trying to defend their cities. And third, some of the illustrations I used in the 2010 edition are irrelevant to the circumstances we face today.

Consequently, I have rewritten much of the book and have added a couple of new chapters that I think you will find interesting. Let the journey begin.

The Prayer

In the midst of the darkest epoch season in human history, Jesus had the audacity to teach us a prayer so powerful that it defies human reason. His words, spoken against the intense backdrop of adversity, would be forever remembered as the Lord's Prayer.

In the midst of Roman oppression, with the reign of the evil emperor Nero within a stone's throw of history, Jesus turned to His tattered brigade of spiritual warriors and said, "Pray that My Father's Kingdom would come and His will be done on earth, as it is in heaven." Was this prayer a sort of "wish upon a star" intended for billions to pray, but only a few to experience in some distant eternity? I don't think so! I think Jesus actually expected us to believe that when we are empowered by the Holy Spirit, we can pull heaven down to earth.

Yet the planet seems to be groaning under the intense pressure of impending doom. The average person today is exposed to more bad news in a week than someone a hundred years ago would have heard in a lifetime. Is the earth eroding, or is it evolving? Is global warming the beginning of the intense heat that will reduce our world to a hot rock spinning hopelessly through space? Will evil finally triumph over good, leaving terrorists to rule our cities as they rape our women, behead our children and execute our men, burying them in mass graves?

Will some maniac dictator finally push the button and blow us into oblivion? What is the answer to the escalating shootings in our public schools, malls and churches?

These are the great questions of our time. These threats press against our very souls, demanding real answers. To compound this sense of urgency, the future of our children depends on us getting this right. I think we can all agree that we will need a multitude of miracles to see the Lord's Prayer answered and our destiny fulfilled.

When Heaven Invades Earth

In his bestselling book *When Heaven Invades Earth* (Destiny Image, 2013), Bill Johnson calls the Body of Christ back to its supernatural roots. He challenges all Christians to walk in signs and wonders, as Jesus so clearly outlined in the Bible, including Mark's gospel:

> He who has believed and has been baptized shall be saved. . . . These signs will accompany those who have believed: in My name they will cast out demons, they will speak with new tongues; they will pick up serpents, and if they drink any deadly poison, it will not hurt them; they will lay hands on the sick, and they will recover.
>
> Mark 16:16–18

Jesus never meant for miracles to be an end in themselves, but rather to be an invitation into a superior Kingdom—a catalyst to cultural transformation fueled by revival. Jesus told the city of Capernaum, "If the miracles had occurred in Sodom which occurred in you, it would have remained to this day" (Matthew 11:23). To the cities of Chorazin and Bethsaida He said, "If the miracles had occurred in Tyre and Sidon which occurred in you, they would have repented long ago in sackcloth and ashes" (verse 21). Our Lord's message is clear: The manifestation of miracles is meant to create a world in revival.

There are some people today who want to remind us that Jesus pronounced judgment over the three cities that did not repent in the New Testament. I would like to point out a couple of things about the judgments of Jesus. First, the only cities Jesus rebuked were towns that had witnessed His incredible miracles. When people experience the supernatural manifestations of the Kingdom of God—when, for instance, the dead are raised, the blind receive their sight, the lame walk, lepers are cleansed and people are delivered from demons—they witness two kingdoms in contrast. This contrast provides them with an opportunity to repent. A Church that does not demonstrate the miraculous works of Christ has failed to give the world this opportunity, and thus has no right to judge people for their lack of response.

Without miracles, the Kingdom of God is reduced to words, concepts and good works. Perceived through this paradigm, the Lions, Rotary and Moose clubs would be the ones contending for first place. While words, concepts and works are important, it is imperative that we demonstrate the power of our great King. When we flood our world with His transforming power, the distinction between darkness and light is obvious and the Lord's Prayer can be answered.

Second, I want to highlight another thing concerning the judgments of Christ. It makes sense that a miracle-working Savior who created the entire world, a sinless Man who needed no mercy, would have strong feelings about the destiny of cities. On the other hand, people like us, who got into the Kingdom through the whipped skin of His back and His nail-scarred hands (and not by our own works), ought to be a little more patient with people who are still lost in darkness. How can we judge cities and ignore the fact that we also deserve to be judged? When we prophesy judgments against cities and nations, we often forget that we are decreeing judgments when we, in fact, need mercy ourselves.

More Than Miracles

Miracles that would have transformed Sodom, Tyre and Sidon did take place in Capernaum, Chorazin and Bethsaida, yet those cities were not transformed. Maybe that is why Jesus said, "He who believes in Me, the works that I do, he will do also; and greater works than these he will do; because I go to the Father" (John 14:12). Without believers demonstrating the miracles of Jesus, the planet will continue to erode into gross darkness that defies explanation. The populace will be reduced to the cesspool of demonic works, leaving hopelessness to encompass the earth like a thick, black cloud.

It is true, therefore, that supernatural works are a major component of revival, but miracles alone don't always lead to city transformation, as Jesus articulated so well in the gospels. So these questions remain: *How* does heaven affect earth in a way that earth becomes like heaven? And what does it look like when God causes the *heavy rain* of His Spirit to be poured out on all flesh? The answers are the subject of this book. May the Lord Himself meet you in its pages and commission you to change the world.

1

Re-forming the Church

Bureaucracy is like setting up scaffolding around a house
to paint the place, and instead painting the scaffolding
for 25 years until the house finally falls down.

Paul Manwaring[1]

love the Church. I can count on two hands the number of
times I have missed a Sunday service in forty years. But many
local congregations have become virtually irrelevant to society. In light of this dilemma, some churches have resorted to
embracing worldly value systems in an effort to become relevant again. This has led to all kinds of confusion. Behaviors
that were clearly deemed sin, wrong and even perversions for
thousands of years not only are now being embraced by much
of the Church, they are even being promoted.

Yet despite this confusion, the fact remains that the Church
is God's mandated agency for world transformation. The Body

of Christ needs another "re-formation," however, so we can be the source of life we were meant to be in this dark world of oppression.

The Parable of the Prodigal Son actually describes the "re-formation" we need. In this parable, two brothers made different choices that led to the same result—separation from their father. Like the Prodigal Son, for some of us "re-formation" will come when we leave the pig farm of our wrong, impoverished thinking and are renewed by the Father's radical love. Only then can we shed the tattered rags of our global orphanage and put on the powerful mantle of God's Royal Family.

Our heavenly Father waits expectantly in our field of dreams, ready to restore us with His *robe of identity*, empower us with His *ring of authority* and give us His understanding with the *sandals of purity*. These things separate us from the defilement of worldly thinking and ensure our true eternal inheritance.

Meanwhile, back at the ranch, many of us, like the Prodigal's elder brother, have forgotten how to celebrate. We have lost sight of our inheritance and have replaced sonship with sacrifice and servanthood. Sacrifice and servanthood are important Kingdom attributes, as long as they embrace and don't replace family values. If the Church is going to be the tipping point of historic exploits, then we must identify old religious paradigms that are hindering the coming Kingdom and then reposition ourselves alongside the Father to welcome the harvest home.

This is a dramatic paradigm shift from the Church in which most of us were raised, but it is being fueled by a changing epoch season in the Kingdom of heaven itself. Let me explain.

From Denominationalism to Apostleships

In 1998, my wife, Kathy, and I moved to Redding, California, to launch the Bethel School of Supernatural Ministry. That same year, I was lying on the floor and praying one morning when the Lord spoke to me so clearly that it stunned me.

He said, *There is a new epoch season emerging in this hour. Much like the Protestant Reformation, there is another reformation coming that will unearth the very foundation of Christianity. This move of the Spirit will absolutely redefine your ideologies and philosophies concerning what the Church is and how she should function.*

I asked Him, *What will this transition look like?*

He said, *My Church is moving from denominationalism to apostleships.*

I actually had no idea what He was talking about, so I asked Him what the difference was between denominationalism and apostleships. He explained to me that in denominationalism, believers gather around doctrinal agreement and divide when they disagree. In apostleships, believers rally around fathers, mothers and families.

The Lord also told me, *I am about to open up the vaults of heaven and reveal depths of My glory that have never before been seen or understood by any living creature.* He explained that this glory was going to be revealed to, and through, His Church in what can only be called a new epoch season. Then He stated, *If I pour out new revelation into the wineskin of denominationalism, it will rip the wineskin and the wine will be lost* (see Luke 5:37–39).

Notice that the Lord used the term *denominationalism* and not *denominations.* The use of "ism" often denotes a distinct ideology, as in communism, racism or humanism. These ideologies are built on distortions of the truth. They are lies sponsored by a diabolical agenda, creating oppression wherever these ideas gain influence.

Personally, I am convinced that the "ism" of denominationalism is an evil spirit. It is every bit as alive in nondenominational churches and some apostolic networks as it is in denominational churches. It is easy to see that denominations have grown up through division, being rooted in the Protestant Reformation of the sixteenth century. We were named Protestants because we were born in a doctrinal protest that continues to this day. (The word *Protestant* originally meant "pro-testament," but soon took on the meaning of "protester.") Both the Protestant Reformation and the movements that have sprung up from it emphasize doctrinal agreement above relationship. This priority has created a culture that constantly threatens to divide people at the very core of their bonding point.

While many believers admit that damaged relationships and church splits are costly, the denominational mindset leads them to conclude that the way to avoid these issues is simply to find ways to enforce doctrinal conformity so disagreements cannot arise. Thus, denominationalism also creates a culture that is critical of anyone who thinks outside the box of tradition, and it desperately fears inspiration.

Leaders under this spirit have more faith in the devil's power to deceive believers than in the Holy Spirit's ability to lead them into all truth. Shepherds in denominationalism resist revelatory thinking because they understand that new ideas spawn disagreements, and disagreement attacks the central nervous system of their churches.

I like to refer to denominationalism as "divided nations," in reference to the way this spirit has infected and limited our ability to disciple the nations. We are called to disciple nations, not to divide people. Note that what I am emphasizing here are the complexities of doctrinal agreement, not the core tenets of faith. The five basic tenets include (1) the Trinity (Father, Son and Holy Spirit); (2) the Person of Jesus Christ (who was born of a virgin, died for our sins, was resurrected and ascended into heaven) as true God and true man; (3) Jesus' visible return for

His Bride; (4) our salvation by grace through faith in Christ; and (5) the inerrant and authoritative nature of Scripture. I also further agree with Bethel Church's statement of faith.[2] Churches don't usually split over these fundamentals. Differences and divisions most often come over issues such as water baptism, speaking in tongues, the nature of leadership, eschatology, money, power, attire and the like.

The Catholic Church

We can gain some great insight by contrasting the Protestant movement with the Catholic Church, which is the mother (like it or not) of the Protestant Church. In fact, let's do a little trivia: How many times has the Catholic Church split in the last two thousand years? The right answer is *three times*. How many times has the Protestant Church split since the Reformation? Harder to count? Okay, I will make the question easier: How many times has the Protestant Church split this month?

One more question: What does the Catholic Church call the leaders of its local churches? The right answer is *father*. The apostle Paul put it this way: "For if you were to have countless tutors in Christ, yet you would not have many fathers, for in Christ Jesus I became your father through the gospel" (1 Corinthians 4:15).

Are you gaining any insight from what these questions reveal? Think about this: Up until the 1960s, Catholic priests preached their sermons in Latin. I think it is easy to see that Catholics were not coming to church to hear a great message, because many of them probably did not even understand the language. As Protestants, we understand the disadvantages of not preaching the Word, and I appreciate that. But why did Catholics go to church? I would like to propose that they were not gathering because they agreed, but because they were (and are) loyal to a family. Is it possible that when Protestants protested bad doctrine at the price of relationship, we came under another curse just as destructive? (It is something to think about.)

Processing Conflict

Belief systems are like accents. All of us speak with an accent, though we often don't realize it until we are in the presence of someone who speaks with an accent different from ours (and of course, we all tend to think it is the other person who has the accent). What most of us don't realize is that we also *see* with an accent. This visual accent is a kind of processing prejudice— a lens—that shapes our view of the world, the Kingdom and the Bible by causing us to see things not *as they are* but *as we believe they are*. Thus, as we live out our faith and read the Bible, we look for and expect to see that which validates what we already believe. In other words, we tend to see only what we are *prepared* to see.

Dr. Lance Wallnau, a respected author and teacher, drove this point home for me at a conference recently. He brought a barrel of varicolored flags up on stage and gave us thirty seconds to count all the gold flags. Then he instructed us to close our eyes, and he asked us how many red flags were in the container. No one could answer the question, of course, because we had only counted the gold flags. This is such a great picture of our tendency to read our own core values, life experiences and doctrinal prejudices into what the Bible says. The danger is that by our selective seeing, we sometimes make the Bible say something it does not say.

The lens of denominationalism is primarily defined by the priority of doctrinal agreement, which necessitates a negative view of disagreement in the Body of Christ. When people with a denominational lens approach Scripture, their selective seeing requires that biblical terms and concepts support the goal of eliminating disagreement, and ultimately, of discouraging individualism.

For example, we see this in the denominational approach to terms like *loyalty* and *unity*. In denominationalism, loyalty is often redefined as "agreeing with the leader." Disagreement is called "disloyalty," and often "disrespect." But the truth is, loyalty is only tested when we don't agree. For instance, David's loyalty to King Saul was revealed not when he lived in the king's house as his favored son-in-law, but when he lived in the wilderness as the king's hated and hunted rival.

Furthermore, if we agree with our leader over an issue, then we are going to do what our leader wants us to do anyway, *because* we agree. It is only when we disagree that the fabric of our relationship is put to the test.

Unity of the Spirit

The *unity of the Spirit* is another great example of a powerful truth that has been reduced to mean "we should all agree on everything so the world will believe there really is a God." Viewing the Bible through the lens of denominationalism redefines the unity of the Spirit to mean "the unity of understanding and agreeing upon the Word." Let's consider one of the premier passages of Scripture on unity—the prayer of Jesus recorded in John 17:

> I do not ask on behalf of these alone, but for those also who believe in Me through their word; *that they may all be one; even as You, Father, are in Me and I in You, that they also may be in Us,* so that the world may believe that You sent Me.
>
> The glory which You have given Me I have given to them, that they may be one, just as We are one; I in them and You in Me, that

they may be perfected in unity, so that the world may know that
You sent Me, and loved them, even as You have loved Me.

John 17:20–23, emphasis added

I have heard many messages on unity in which this passage
is used to exhort believers to get along. But did you notice that,
contrary to popular opinion, the unity Jesus prayed for in this
passage is not the unity between believers, but the unity between
a believer and God? Look closely at His prayer. Jesus petitioned
the Father "that they may all be one; even as You, Father, are in
Me and I in You, that *they also may be in Us*" (verse 21, emphasis added). It is easy to assume that "all be one" refers to being
one with each other, but Jesus defines it as being one with God.

Now look at this part of the next two verses: ". . . just as We
are one; *I in them* and You in Me, that they may be perfected
in unity" (emphasis added). Again, the key emphasis here is
"I in them." Nowhere does Jesus pray that we should be "in"
each other.

It does not seem to occur to most of us that Jesus could
not even get His twelve disciples to get along with each other
when He walked the earth with them. But when we read these
verses with denominational mindsets, we need to see selectively
that Jesus is praying against disagreements, because these days,
disagreement equals church splits. In reading with our visual
accent here, we miss one of the most powerful truths in the
Bible. God wants to be one with His people! The prayer that
Jesus prayed in John 17 is actually an extension of the talk He
had earlier with His disciples, in John 14. Let's check it out:

He who has seen Me has seen the Father; how can you say, "Show
us the Father"? Do you not believe that I am in the Father, and
the Father is in Me? The words that I say to you I do not speak
on My own initiative, but the Father abiding in Me does His
works. Believe Me that I am in the Father and the Father is in

Me; otherwise believe because of the works themselves. Truly, truly, I say to you, he who believes in Me, the works that I do, he will do also; and greater works than these he will do; because I go to the Father.

John 14:9–12

Jesus told His guys, "If you've seen Me, you've seen the Father." We know for a fact that Jesus was not saying that He is the Father, because another Voice from heaven said, "This is My beloved Son, in whom I am well-pleased" when Jesus was baptized (Matthew 3:17). Jesus was not talking to Himself there. And in John 14, He was simply making the point that He and the Father are an inseparable unity.

Think about it this way: If you mix red paint and blue paint, you get the color purple. Every time you see purple, you know it is the manifestation of these two primary colors. But I defy you to separate them once they are mixed. The Father and the Son are the manifestation of a celestial union that transcends human rationalization or finite explanation.

Jesus said the works (miracles) He did were signs of the Father's presence working through Him. This tells us that, while we may not be able to *explain* the nature of this union, we can *experience* it. But wait, it gets even better. Jesus shocks us with this next decree: "He who believes in Me, the works that I do, he will do also; and greater works than these he will do" (John 14:12).

Now let's put this all together. Jesus prayed in John 17 that the Body of Christ would be united with the Godhead in the same way that He Himself is united with His Father. The implication is that when people *see us*, they have *seen the Father*. And if they don't believe us on account of our words, they should believe us on account of our works, because we are to do greater works than Jesus did. That is the kind of unity that will cause the world to know that the Kingdom of God has come near them!

2

::::::::::::::::::::::::::::::::::

The Kingdom Is a Family Affair

Unity is not conformity, but the celebration of diversity.

Source Unknown

Jesus taught us to pray, "*Our Father* who is in heaven . . ." He did not say to pray, "Our God in heaven . . ." The Kingdom is a family affair. God is our Father, and our Savior is His Son, and we are the Bride of Christ. To mirror heaven, therefore, the Church must be built on family values and relational connections. That is why apostleships are so very important. Apostles create *covenantal, family* relationships because believers are attached to and through *fathers, mothers and family*, not doctrine. This promotes freedom for people to think creatively, to dream, to envision with God and to experience new depths of the Holy Spirit. This relational security creates an environment that attracts revelation. The very nature of revelation is that people get fresh perspectives and deeper insights from God's

Word *and* have extraordinary encounters with the supernatural Kingdom of God.

Disagreement does exist in apostolic cultures; in fact, you could say that the culture even encourages it, or certainly allows it, by inviting revelation. Doctrinal disputes often arise as believers process fresh truth that frequently assails old, traditional mindsets. But the unity of the *Spirit* (not unity of the word) is the foundation of apostleships, because the priority of relationships is kept above doctrinal agreement, which promotes highly relational core connections.

In our apostolic culture, we must therefore maintain strong, respectful and loving connections with one another as we work through these revelatory insights. Revelation has always been the child of relationship more than it is the fruit of intense study. Jesus put it this way: "No longer do I call you slaves, for the slave does not know what his master is doing; but I have called you friends, for all things that I have heard from My Father I have made known to you" (John 15:15).

Relating to God as a slave keeps us in the Dark Ages when it comes to understanding the Father's business. But friendship with God unlocks the heavenly vault of His secrets, exposing treasures that have been hidden in Him from eternity. Moses indicated that revelation belongs to a relational context when he wrote, "The secret things belong to the LORD our God, but the things revealed belong to us and to our sons forever" (Deuteronomy 29:29).

When God reveals His Kingdom secrets to us, they become part of our ancestral dynasty, which is to be passed down from generation to generation, much like a family business or a plot of land. Doctrinal insights were meant to be carried relationally, not discovered in the think tanks of denominational seminaries. We see this in the life of Joshua, who received wisdom from fatherly impartation when Moses laid his hands on him.

Deuteronomy 34:9 says, "Now Joshua the son of Nun was filled with the spirit of wisdom, for Moses had laid his hands on him."

About the Father's Business

I am not saying that doctrinal agreement is not important in the Church. It is important, but it simply does not hold the place of primacy. I like to illustrate the importance of correctly ordering our priorities by looking at the product sales industry, in which two of the main business divisions have competing core values. There is the manufacturing division, which typically has a "zero defect" core value, and there is the research and development (R&D) division, which has a "discovery by trial and error" core value.

When Apple Inc. went to market with its first iPhone, the goal of the manufacturing department was to have no defects whatsoever in the phones being sold. On the other hand, the R&D department, which invented the iPhone, probably made hundreds of mistakes in the process of developing the product. If Apple tried to apply the same core values to its R&D department as it does to its manufacturing division, it would never invent any products. Eventually, this would result in Apple having nothing to bring to market, and soon it would be forced into bankruptcy.

In other words, even though both of these divisions are part of the same great company, success in these two departments is measured much differently. Mistakes are the inevitable process of invention, but they are the demise of production. In spiritual terms, the priority of agreement in denominationalism creates a "no defects" policy that makes little or no room for the discovery process that empowers innovation, invention and revelation. When truth is not processed perfectly the first time, the entire revelation is usually discarded as "heresy" or maligned as "dangerous."

A branch of Christianity called the Shepherding movement is a great example of this. This movement was birthed through some incredible revelation and insights into fatherhood, discipleship, authority and accountability. But many among the leadership of this movement used these truths to control believers instead of empowering them. Consequently, the larger Church threw out the entire revelation as unbiblical, which has greatly hindered progress in these important areas.

Two other cases in point are the Latter Rain movement and the Manifest Sons of God movement. Christians who were a part of these movements had some real insights into the true identity of believers. But many of the movement leaders began using their insights to promote spiritual elitism, and the entire revelation was branded as heretical.

The "no defects" policy of denominationalism is a problem, for one, because we are applying it to the wrong area. Our individual character and our relationship with God and others are the things that belong in the manufacturing department, so to speak. These are the areas in which we should strive for zero defects. The R&D department of the Church includes learning to apply truth, digging deeper into the Word, experimenting with the Holy Spirit, moving in the gifts, stepping out in faith, dreaming with God, attempting the impossible, believing the unreasonable and so on. (Of course, both departments exist in the same people, so the illustration breaks down a bit here.)

In reality, we must learn to balance the priorities of risk-taking and excellence in all areas of life—in our character development, in our relationships and in our pursuit of revelation. The problem is that risk-taking creates messes, exposes flaws and, more often than not, teaches us what *does not work*. But this is the process that leads to true spiritual maturity.

It is essential that we in the Body of Christ develop and embrace an attitude of risk, or soon we will be eating old, worm-infested manna. If we are to be the light of the world, we must start emanating who God is through cutting-edge Kingdom insights, and we must stop reflecting the world's outdated, stale philosophies and strategies that for the most part are simply repackaged traditional mindsets. God is the same yesterday, today and forever (see Hebrews 13:8), but what He is doing in the world is not static. He is always moving forward.

The Risky Life of the Kingdom

When we look closely at the beginning of creation, we see that God Himself is a risk-taker. He did not childproof the Garden; instead, He planted two trees there—the Tree of Life and the Tree of the Knowledge of Good and Evil. The latter would kill a man within 24 hours of eating its fruit (see Genesis 2:17). God gave man the chance to live forever, but only at the risk of the death penalty.

Let's look at another great example of the risky life of the Kingdom. Jesus went to a wedding party with His twelve guys and His mother. After they had partied for a long time, they ran out of wine. Mary pressed her Son into making more wine. (I always wonder how Mary knew Jesus could make wine, unless He was making wine at home.) John records the incident in his gospel:

> When the headwaiter tasted the water which had become wine, and did not know where it came from (but the servants who had drawn the water knew), the headwaiter called the bridegroom, and said to him, "Every man serves the good wine first, and when the people have drunk freely, then he serves the poorer wine; but you have kept the good wine until now."
>
> John 2:9–10

The expression "drunk freely" in this passage is translated from the Greek word *methuo*. It means "to be drunk or intoxicated." Jesus made wine for people who were already drunk! No, God was not condoning drunkenness. There is no way the Lord wanted people to get drunk; the Bible makes that clear in several other passages (see Ephesians 5:18; Galatians 5:20–21). But God does not control people. In fact, He actually provides options and then empowers people to make great choices. When we make the right choices, He rewards us. If God were to take away our bad choices, He would remove the possibility of a reward for good choices.

Denominationalism produces cultural sanitization by eliminating people's choices through religious control. Shepherds in this culture are charged with teaching people *what* to think, not *how* to think. When people exercise their power to choose, whatever is inside of them—good, bad or ugly—has an opportunity to manifest. But most denominational cultures are simply unequipped to help people face the reality of who they are and empower them to take responsibility for their messes without controlling them.

Apostles, on the other hand, value risk because they understand that faith requires risk. Only a culture driven by risk-taking faith can produce life. Consequently, a high level of freedom exists in apostolic meetings and cultures, allowing believers to be extremely powerful or sadly pitiful. In order to preserve this freedom, apostolic cultures develop strategic, empowering ways to help people take responsibility for their choices and clean up their messes. (We will talk more about this later in the book.)

I have always found it easy to identify people who grew up in denominationalism, because they refuse to think for themselves. They are accustomed to their leaders doing all their thinking for them. I experienced this a couple of years ago in our School of Supernatural Ministry. We had just begun the school year, and I was teaching a fresh group of two hundred students. That day, I was exhorting them to take risks in God and not worry about failing. As I shared, I allowed the students to ask questions.

A young man raised his hand and asked, "You're not talking about moral failure, are you?"

"Of course not," I responded.

I continued teaching, and a few minutes later his hand went up again.

"Johnny, do you have another question?"

"Yes," he said, looking like a lost puppy dog. "You're not saying that we should do things like jump off a roof by faith and see if God will catch us, are you?"

"No!" I said, a little impatient this time. "And I'm not trying to convince you to drink poisoned Kool-Aid or wait for flying saucers, either!"

Johnny went on to ask about five more questions in that session, all of them in the same vein. With every question, I grew more frustrated. (I used to say that there is no such thing as a stupid question. Johnny convinced me that I was wrong about that.)

Finally, in complete exasperation, I paused and said, "Okay, everyone. Ready? Turn on your brains! You have permission to think! If I say something that can be taken five different ways, please process it in the only way that makes sense as a Christian."

As the months passed, I got to know Johnny better. I discovered that he had been brought up in a Christian home where his parents did all the thinking for him. To make matters worse, he was part of a church in which the pastor taught with the assumption that his people were stupid. This leader would painstakingly and methodically explain each of his points, closing all the wrong theological and philosophical doors, as if the room were filled with complete idiots. Consequently, Johnny's mind was reduced to memorizing and repeating facts. He had never learned how to process information or think for himself. The fear of being wrong had imprisoned his intellect and crushed his imagination.

Leaders in denominationalism tend to preach to convince people of truth. They seem to be under the impression that it is their responsibility to persuade people what to believe. Leaders in apostleships preach to inspire and encourage their people, understanding that while they are responsible to preach the Bible, it is the Holy Spirit's responsibility to lead people into all truth (see John 16:13). Apostolic leaders prize the relationship that believers have with the Holy Spirit. They train people to be dependent on the Holy Spirit because, ultimately, He is the one responsible for their maturity in Christ.

Relating to the Word

The goal of the Bible has always been to bring us into an encounter and a relationship with God (see John 17:3). Yet if knowing the Word and knowing God were synonymous, then the scribes and Pharisees, who memorized the entire Old Testament, would have been the first people to recognize Christ. But their very approach to the Scriptures set them up for spiritual blindness. They abandoned the true purpose for studying the Word by exchanging a relationship with God for academic arguments, and they never demanded that their theology lead to an encounter with Him.

Someone might argue that if you base your relationship with God on an experience, you could be deceived. That is so true. But on the other hand, if you study the Bible and it does not lead you into an encounter with the Almighty, then you are already deceived.

The moment theologians abandon a relationship with God as being their *primary* mission in understanding the Bible, they have already begun to enter into deception. This is true of anybody else, too. Paul described these people best when writing to Timothy. He said that they have "a form of godliness, although they have denied its power" and that they are "always learning and never able to come to the knowledge of the truth" (2 Timothy 3:5, 7).

In a sense, the Bible is like the owner's manual in a new car. You read the manual, expecting to understand how to operate your automobile and take care of it. If you memorize the manual and still cannot operate the car, what purpose would there be in reading the manual? Often, however, you read the owner's manual and you still don't quite understand how a certain feature functions until you try it out yourself with the manual in hand. You need to encounter and experience it firsthand to really grasp it well.

Can you imagine what it would be like if the owner of a car lost sight of the fact that the goal of reading the owner's manual is not to memorize it, but to learn to effectively operate the automobile? Wouldn't it be strange if someone could quote the entire manual, but never wanted to drive the car? Yet people do this with the Bible all the time. It has become commonplace for people to memorize Bible verses without even having the desire to experience what they put to memory.

An apostolic culture deals with deception primarily through relational accountability and spiritual discernment rather than through intellectualism. For example, when the apostles in the early Church struggled over doctrinal issues, they compared their understanding of the Scriptures with their experience in God in order to come to their conclusions about the truth. Let's look at one example in the book of Acts:

> Some of the sect of the Pharisees who had believed stood up, saying, "It is necessary to circumcise them and to direct them to observe the Law of Moses."

The apostles and the elders came together to look into this matter. After there had been much debate, Peter stood up and said to them, "Brethren, you know that in the early days God made a choice among you, that by my mouth the Gentiles would hear the word of the gospel and believe. And God, who knows the heart, testified to them giving them the Holy Spirit, just as He also did to us; and He made no distinction between us and them, cleansing their hearts by faith. Now therefore why do you put God to the test by placing upon the neck of the disciples a yoke which neither our fathers nor we have been able to bear? But we believe that we are saved through the grace of the Lord Jesus, in the same way as they also are."

All the people kept silent, and they were listening to Barnabas and Paul as they were relating what signs and wonders God had done through them among the Gentiles.

After they had stopped speaking, James answered, saying, "Brethren, listen to me. Simeon has related how God first concerned Himself about taking from among the Gentiles a people for His name. With this the words of the Prophets agree, just as it is written, 'After these things I will return, and I will rebuild the tabernacle of David which has fallen, and I will rebuild its ruins, and I will restore it, so that the rest of mankind may seek the LORD, and all the Gentiles who are called by My name, says the LORD, who makes these things known from long ago.' Therefore it is my judgment that we do not trouble those who are turning to God from among the Gentiles, but that we write to them that they abstain from things contaminated by idols and from fornication and from what is strangled and from blood."

Acts 15:5–20

Notice that the apostles took Peter's experience with the Gentiles, and also the testimonies of Paul and Barnabas's signs and wonders, into the debate to determine what their doctrinal stance should be concerning how the Law applied to the Gentiles. Apostleships most often value the voice of the Holy Spirit (see Acts 15:28) and God-experiences above academic arguments. They also tend to process first from their hearts, rather than from their heads. I don't at all mean to communicate that apostleships are intellectually shallow or mindlessly motivated. I am simply pointing out that the Spirit directs apostles, and so they often find themselves living beyond the boundaries of human logic and reason (though not, of course, outside the counsel of the Scriptures).

A disciple who is following an apostolic leadership team will be required to exercise a high level of faith and trust, as well as extreme discernment, because the structures, strategies, vision and mission of apostleships tend to be Spirit-inspired. By their very nature, apostles don't give preeminence to "common sense." I call this approach *spirategies*, meaning "Spirit-led strategies." It is the spiritual process of developing an apostolic mission.

This way of approaching life in the Kingdom is not new. It is demonstrated throughout the entire Bible. From Gideon's army of three hundred pitcher-carrying soldiers, to Elisha's floating axe head, to Joshua's seven-day march around an enemy city, the Word of God is filled with irrational stories that defy common reason. Church leaders who have denominational mindsets often share these stories as awesome historic events of the God who does the unreasonable, the irrational and the impossible. But it never occurs to some of them that He still requires His people to trust Him in living a life that transcends our understanding, and that He invites us into His miraculous interventions today.

This resistance in some leaders to experiencing the impossible interventions of God has resulted in many believers being educated out of obedience. They have exchanged God's works for good deeds, reducing "Jesus people" to being only nice, friendly citizens instead of being fire-breathing world changers. They have tried to domesticate the Lion of the tribe of Judah, attempting to reduce Him to a circus animal.

3

::::::::::::::::::::::::::::::::::

From a Hierarchy
to an Heir-archy

The Bible is not a road map; it is a compass.

Source Unknown

It is time for us to leave the circus of the Church as we have organized it and take our heavenly seat with Christ. But we have to leave the slave camp of denominationalism to be joint heirs with Jesus. The apostle Paul's letter to the Romans says it best:

For all who are being led by the Spirit of God, these are sons of God. For you have not received a spirit of slavery leading to fear again, but you have received a spirit of adoption as sons by which we cry out, "Abba! Father!" The Spirit Himself testifies with our spirit that we are children of God, and if children, heirs also, heirs of God and fellow heirs with Christ, if indeed we suffer with Him so that we may also be glorified with Him.

Romans 8:14–17

Paul points out that we are no longer slaves, but are adopted sons in which we now relate to God as our Daddy (the Aramaic word *Abba*). Because our heavenly Father is also the King of the world, through inheritance we are heirs of the throne. It is important for us to understand that we received this promotion through adoption and not on the basis of our abilities. The ramifications of this royal nepotistic transition is that we are moving from a hierarchical leadership model to an heirarchy, as we are heirs with Christ to the throne of God (see Revelation 3:21).

Denominationalism is based on hierarchies. Hierarchies are most often developed through a pecking order. In a henhouse, chickens organize their society by pecking each other in order to determine the top chicken, the bottom chicken and all the chickens in between. In other words, you could say that hierarchies are structures determined by the level of dominance a chicken has in the henhouse, or in this case, a person has in an organization.

Denominationalism is a highly developed henhouse where leaders receive authority based on their performance. They go to a seminary, earn a degree and become a pastor. The trouble with achievement-based authority is that it creates a performance-driven leadership culture where the most accomplished person is commissioned to lead. (There is nothing wrong with education or seminaries, as long as they are not the ultimate qualifiers for leadership.) Because this type of leadership is primarily derived through works, anybody who outperforms his or her leader is a threat to the organization. The culture itself is therefore either subconsciously or proactively designed to undermine or sabotage (peck) anyone who is more accomplished than the leader. In this way, the leader's floor becomes the followers' ceiling.

On the other hand, apostleships are heir-archies. In heir-archies, leaders are not determined based on their ability to perform, but based on the level of favor they have received from God (Daddy) through their relationship with Him as a son or daughter. Apostolic leaders receive authority not based on *what* they know, but based on *whom* they know. This is what I term *called-based* leadership.

Jesus, for example, *called* each of His disciples without regard to their educational qualifications or ministry experience. Here is the passage where the Lord enlisted the "Sons of Thunder," as He affectionately called them (in Mark 3:17):

> Going on from there He saw two other brothers, James the son of Zebedee, and John his brother, in the boat with Zebedee their father, mending their nets; and He called them.
>
> Matthew 4:21

Even the apostle Paul, who was extremely well educated and was a highly qualified religious leader, said that God called him by His grace:

> But when God, who had set me apart even from my mother's womb and called me through His grace, was pleased to reveal His Son in me so that I might preach Him among the Gentiles, I did not immediately consult with flesh and blood, nor did I go up to Jerusalem to those who were apostles before me; but I went away to Arabia, and returned once more to Damascus.
>
> Galatians 1:15–17

The Bible describes grace as the unmerited favor of God toward people—the key word here being *unmerited*. Leaders in apostleships are not necessarily uneducated, inexperienced or weak, yet they are not put into leadership primarily because of their qualifications or their pedigree. Instead, they are installed as leaders because God chooses them. When God calls a person to lead, He releases favor on them. His favor qualifies them. The commissioning of Joshua is a great illustration of this:

> The LORD said to Moses, "Take Joshua the son of Nun, a man in whom is the Spirit, and lay your hand on him; and have him stand before Eleazar the priest and before all the congregation, and commission him in their sight. You shall put some of your authority on him, in order that all the congregation of the sons of Israel may obey him."
>
> Numbers 27:18–20

We know that Joshua was the most qualified person to take Moses' place because he had served as his second-in-command for years. But God did not mention Joshua's experience. Instead, He reminded Moses that Joshua had the Spirit on him. The Spirit qualified Joshua to lead the people. God then instructed Moses to lay his hands on him and give him some of his authority. The Hebrew word for *authority* here is also translated "splendor" nine times, "majesty" six times and "beauty" or "glory" twice. True God-appointed leaders carry a certain majesty, splendor or favor about them that causes people to recognize their authority and want to follow them.

Mantles and Missions

When God commissions leaders, as He did with Joshua, He releases *mantles* over them. These mantles give them the supernatural ability to complete their mission. Unlike the gifts and calls of God that remain on a person for life, a *mantle* stays with the *mission*, not with the man. For example, anyone who becomes president of the United States must be very gifted. A person does not rise to the highest office in our land without that qualification. But on Inauguration Day, something powerful takes place in the spirit realm; a presidential mantle from heaven is given to that person. God never grants someone an assignment without giving him or her the ability to complete it.

God Himself establishes all authority in the universe. Every leadership role on the planet is therefore a mission from God (see Romans 13:1). The presidential mantle gives these leaders the capacity to direct our country beyond their human ability. When their term is over and they leave the White House, however, the mantle stays with the mission so it can be passed on to the next president. But their leadership gifts and calling remain with them.

Joshua is a great example of how mantles enhance a person's ability to carry out his or her mission. Before Joshua ever received his own mantle, he had the chance to experience the effects of the mantle that rested on the shoulders of Moses. We find one of the most striking examples of this in Exodus 17, the story of Moses commissioning Joshua to take his soldiers and go down in the valley to fight Amalek. During the battle, Moses went up on the mountain and held up his hands. When Moses got tired and dropped his arms, Joshua began to lose the battle. When Moses lifted up his arms, Joshua won. It became clear to the Israelite leadership that Joshua's victory was directly related to Moses raising his hands, so they put a leader on each side of Moses to help support his arms until Joshua won the battle and defeated Amalek (see Exodus 17:8–13).

If we don't understand how to recognize and align ourselves under true spiritual authority, we may build bigger armies, develop better strategies and buy more powerful weapons, but we will still lose. It just never occurs to us that if we support (honor) our leaders, we will inherit their victories. Yet this is how leadership is designed to work in an apostleship. The honor between leaders and those who follow them creates a relationship in which the leaders' ceiling becomes the followers' floor.

4

Apostle Covering and Angel Help

Those who danced looked quite insane to those who couldn't hear the music.

Friedrich Nietzsche

When Moses raised his arms on the top of that mountain, Joshua routed the enemy army. But what actually made Joshua successful that day? What really happened to the enemy's army that caused them suddenly to go from victory to defeat? That is the multimillion-dollar question, because if we could bottle success, we could change the world.

I think I have the answer to Joshua's success, although it would not fit in a bottle. I believe angels helped Joshua defeat the enemy when Aaron and Hur held up Moses' hands.

Let me explain it like this. The book of Revelation gives us some great insights into the way apostolic authority functions in the invisible realm. Jesus said to the apostle John,

> To the angel of the church in Ephesus write:
> The One who holds the seven stars in His right hand, the One who walks among the seven golden lampstands, says this:
> "I know your deeds and your toil and perseverance, and that you cannot tolerate evil men, and you put to the test those who call themselves apostles, and they are not, and you found them to be false; and you have perseverance and have endured for My name's sake, and have not grown weary."
>
> Revelation 2:1–3

In Revelation 1:4 and 11 Jesus commissioned John to write seven letters that became the apostolic mandates for seven different churches throughout Asia. But did you catch the fact that John was not told to write the letters to the natural leaders of those churches? Instead, he was instructed to write the letters to the seven angels of the seven churches. Wow! What we learn from these letters is astonishing. We see that true apostolic ministries have angels assigned to them. These angels are commissioned to carry out the mission dictated by a particular apostle's mandate and *metron*. The word *metron* means the realm or boundaries of a leader's spiritual influence (see Romans 12:3; 2 Corinthians 10:13). In this case, John had authority over seven specific geographic regions, so he had seven angels assigned to him.

It is my personal conviction that one of the essential elements that has ushered in this apostolic age is that the angels no longer recognize the performance-based authority of denominationalism. Paul teaches us that angels recognize true spiritual authority. In fact, it is the angels who answer our prayers and fulfill our prophecies. Angels are mentioned more than 180 times in the New Testament alone. Where have all the angels gone in the twenty-first-century Church? What would the world be like if we were suddenly to employ angelic help on this planet in the same degree as they did in the first century? I think that as we are reformed into this new apostolic wineskin, we are about to find out.

Apostolic Covering

The Holy Spirit commissioned the apostle Paul, and the apostles at Jerusalem sent him out (see Acts 15:22–25). Subsequently, Paul's ministry witnessed the effectiveness of being under a covering that comes from submission to true spiritual authority. The difference between people who are under authority and those who are not is evident in the contrast we see between the Jewish priest Sceva's sons and Paul's ministry. The demonic realm did not even recognize the authority of the sons of Sceva:

> God was performing extraordinary miracles by the hands of Paul, so that handkerchiefs or aprons were even carried from his body to the sick, and the diseases left them and the evil spirits went out. But also some of the Jewish exorcists, who went from place to place, attempted to name over those who had the evil spirits the name of the Lord Jesus, saying, "I adjure you by Jesus whom Paul preaches." Seven sons of one Sceva, a Jewish chief priest, were doing this. And the evil spirit answered and said to them, "I recognize Jesus, and I know about Paul, but who are you?" And the man, in whom was the evil spirit, leaped on them and subdued all of them and overpowered them, so that they fled out of that house naked and wounded.
>
> Acts 19:11–16

It is amazing that an apostle's hankie had more power than seven sons of Sceva using Jesus' name did. It is hard to imagine that demons recognized Paul's handkerchief and left people's bodies, but refused to depart when this priest's seven sons tried to cast them out using the name of Jesus. But that is what happened. (Maybe there are such things as apostolic hankies. . . .) The demon's words were quite startling: "I recognize Jesus, and we know about Paul, but who are you?" (verse 15). When we come into submission to God's apostolic leaders, we are known in heaven and feared in hell. True heavenly authority causes angels to help us and causes demons to respect our influence.

Because he was a man under authority, even the Gentile centurion in the book of Luke recognized that Jesus had the authority to heal his sick servant:

> Now Jesus started on His way with them; and when He was not far from the house, the centurion sent friends, saying to Him, "Lord, do not trouble Yourself further, for I am not worthy for You to come under my roof; for this reason I did not even consider myself worthy to come to You, but just say the word, and my servant will be healed. For I also am a man placed under authority, with soldiers under me; and I say to this one, 'Go!' and he goes, and to another, 'Come!' and he comes, and to my slave, 'Do this!' and he does it." Now when Jesus heard this, He marveled at him, and turned and said to the crowd that was following Him, "I say to you, not even in Israel have I found such great faith."
>
> Luke 7:6–9

This is how true spiritual authority functions. We come in *sub*mission to the Father's mission and we get *com*missioned. Legitimate, anointed leaders carry an apostolic mission and are responsible to commission the Body of Christ.

Even Jesus Himself said, "For I have come down from heaven, not to do My own will, but the will of Him who sent Me" (John 6:38). Likewise, He said, "I can do nothing on My own initiative. As I hear, I judge; and My judgment is just, because

I do not seek My own will, but the will of Him who sent Me" (John 5:30). Was Jesus actually saying, "I really didn't want to do this miracle and redemption stuff. This is all My Father's idea"? No! He was simply demonstrating how apostles ("sent ones") receive authority. They yield their will to God and allow Him to carry out His plan through their lives and the lives of those over whom they have authority. Like the twelve disciples Jesus sent out to spread the Kingdom, we also need to be sent, not just go.

As we have seen, God has also commissioned angels to partner with His leaders in fulfilling their apostolic mission. When we are under God's authority, which includes being under His appointed leaders, we also partner with the angelic hosts. Hebrews 1:14 says of the angels, "Are they not all ministering spirits, sent out to render service for the sake of those who will inherit salvation?" The responsibility of the angels is to make sure that the sons and daughters of the King come into their divine destinies and fulfill the mission of the Kingdom.

Commissioning Angels

As I alluded to already, one of the most common ways angels are commissioned is through prayer and prophecy. Consider the words of the psalmist:

> Bless the LORD, you His angels, mighty in strength, who *perform His word, obeying the voice of His word!* Bless the LORD, all you His hosts, you who serve Him, doing His will. Bless the LORD, all you works of His, in all places of His dominion; bless the LORD, O my soul!
>
> Psalm 103:20–22, emphasis added

The angels heed the voice of His word. The Church is His voice that declares His word on earth. I don't think this means that we have to tell the angels what to do; I simply am saying that when we pray and prophesy in the name of the Lord, the angels hear the word of the Lord and go out to perform it. But we can only declare a word of the Lord that commissions and sends the angels if we are under authority and therefore have authority.

We find another indication of the nature and power of spiritual authority in a statement Stephen made before he was stoned. He stood before his accusers and recounted a *Reader's Digest* version of the Old Testament, including the history of how Israel came to be enslaved in Egypt:

> There arose another king over Egypt who knew nothing about Joseph. It was he who took shrewd advantage of our race and mistreated our fathers so that they would expose their infants and they would not survive.
>
> Acts 7:18–19

It is important to note that Stephen did not say there arose a king who knew not God and tried to destroy their race. Rather, he said there arose a king who knew nothing about Joseph. Joseph's personal victories had brought him into a position of favor and authority, which released a corporate covering over his family.

You have probably heard the story—Joseph's extended family, who believed he was dead, came to Egypt in search of food. When his brothers, the ones who had sold him into slavery, found out that Joseph was alive, they begged him for their lives. He told them that what they had meant for evil, God used for good. He forgave them and invited them to move to Egypt so they would be safe from the famine. Seventy members of his family relocated there, where Pharaoh gave them the best land. They multiplied and spread all over the nation, growing prosperous and remaining free. The Israelites lived a life of incredible blessing during the years of Joseph's rule, not because they deserved it, but because Joseph did (see Genesis 37; 39–48).

Why did Joseph deserve this blessing? What qualified him to carry such authority and favor? It was not his intelligence, education, charisma, people skills or any other quality by which we humans generally judge a person's leadership ability. Joseph rose to prominence for three reasons: (1) He lived supernaturally, as demonstrated through his ability to interpret dreams; (2) in a dream he was called to be a leader by God Himself; and (3) he passed every test of his character on the way to his calling. Divine callings, proven character and a supernatural lifestyle are the three primary marks of a person with true spiritual authority.

Covering and Accountability

There is a difference between covering and accountability. Real accountability is only present in our lives when we have a personal relationship with people who can and do speak into our hearts, our circumstances and our relationships. Everyone needs these deep covenant connections—not primarily because they keep us from failing, but because they inspire us to reach for the high call of God that rests on each of our lives. Historically, accountability has majored in helping people restrain their bad behavior. But as new creatures in Christ, we all need to be accountable to people who regularly remind us that we were born to make history. (That is why it is called account-ability, not account-disability.)

It is very unlikely that leaders who carry the apostolic mantles providing the covering for entire movements will be able to provide relational accountability for most of the people under their covering. The very nature of their corporate responsibility prevents them from having the necessary time it takes to cultivate deep relationships with that many people, yet that kind of time and relationship are paramount in order for real discipleship and/or accountability to take place. When it comes to leaders who operate in these apostolic roles, however, the truth of Proverbs 18:24 applies: "A man of too many friends comes to ruin."

It is therefore important for believers to find accountability among the people they are doing life with (rather than looking to leaders who would not have the necessary time). You don't need someone famous to provide you with accountability; you just need a wise person who has time for you and is willing to speak honestly into your life. It should be a person you highly respect, who believes in you and has more experience than you. Being accountable to your peers can be helpful, but it seldom has the impact that a more experienced person can have on your life.

Perhaps as you read this chapter, the idea that someone has authority over us in God feels painful at best and impossible at worst. I know those feelings well, having grown up with two stepfathers who abused their authority in my life. But the benefits of having true spiritual leadership in our lives far outweigh the internal struggle it takes to get there. And for many believers, it is a struggle. Some people who seem to have the greatest resistance to the concept of spiritual authority would not dare tell even their unsaved employer, "You can't tell me what to do. The Lord is my Shepherd; I don't submit to earthly authority." Instead, they arrive at work at whatever time their boss tells them. They wear whatever uniform the corporate code demands. They carry out the tasks that are required of them five or six days a week. But on Sunday, they come to church and refuse to work in the nursery or perform some simple job that leadership asks them to do. I have had believers tell me that the Shepherding movement of the 1970s or some church leader hurt them, so they will never submit to spiritual authority again. Their life message is clear: "You can't tell me what to do." Can you imagine what your income would be like if you extended that way of thinking into the marketplace? It troubles me when Christians will do for money what they will not do for love.

Of course, there is always "spiritual leadership" in the Body of Christ who think it is their responsibility to control people instead of empowering them to fulfill their God-given mandate. Such leaders use fear and manipulation to get their flock to do what is needed. These kinds of people should not be leaders, and others should not trust them or submit to them. True apostles always include the fulfillment of their people's dreams as part of their primary mission from God. Whenever shepherds lead in a way that does not significantly benefit their people, they are misusing their authority. In fact, the first group of people a leader is called to minister to is his or her own family. Scripture is clear that the foundation of a leader's authority is in managing family relationships at home (see 1 Timothy 3:1–5). Many leaders have forgotten Paul's exhortation and have sacrificed their families on the altar of public ministry.

It is imperative that fathers and mothers teach their sons and daughters to sacrifice. Sacrifice is part of life in the Kingdom. But there is a huge difference between making a sacrifice and being sacrificed to obtain some "God-given purpose." If I could get a million people saved in Africa but it cost me one of my children, I would choose to keep my child. If I chose to throw one of my kids under the bus to obtain some ministry goal, no matter how lofty the vision, my ministry would be built on a rotten foundation. I grieve for the children of many leaders and wonder what those people are thinking by neglecting and mishandling their primary responsibilities. Let me be clear: This is not the kind of leader I am suggesting that you trust. Yet there is no such thing as a perfect leader, except for Jesus. We cannot require perfection from any leader, but we can expect those who lead us to demonstrate maturity, to love us and to live humbly.

The Move to Apostolic Families

I believe that much of the Church in our day is making a dramatic transition out of denominationalism and into apostolic families. This is often referred to as the emerging apostolic age.

That is, in fact, the title of the next chapter. In the pages ahead, we will contrast the nature of traditional pastoral government with that of an apostolic structure. This will help us gain more insight into this new season we are entering.

It is paramount in this new season that we clearly understand the apostles' mantle and mandate to transform culture. With this fresh revelation, we can lay governmental foundations in the Church that empower, rather than restrain, today's apostles in their extraordinary calling.

5

‌

The Emerging Apostolic Age

In times of change, learners inherit the Earth, while the learned find themselves beautifully equipped to deal with a world that no longer exists.

Eric Hoffer[1]

It was early Sunday morning, and the Bethel Church leadership team gathered, as we do every week, to pray for God to move miraculously among us. The atmosphere was charged as the small room filled up with about thirty passionate staff members, all eager for their chance to lead out in prayer. Each leader stood with anticipation, like racehorses waiting for the gate to open. My turn was near, so I formed my thoughts as the person next to me concluded his fervent exhortation.

I was just about to blurt out, "I release the pool of Bethesda over Bethel Church," when the Lord suddenly interrupted my thinking. *That's an old prophetic word!* He said.

I was stunned. I quickly reminded the Lord that just six months earlier, He had told me that the Church was like the pool of Bethesda. But now He was indicating that this word was old manna.

Lord, how could this be an old word? I questioned.

That's an old word! the Lord repeated.

What's the new word? I asked, a bit sheepishly.

My Church is moving from the pool of Bethesda to Ezekiel's river, He said.

I had no idea what the Lord meant by that, but I quickly gathered my thoughts while the team waited, and then I boldly pronounced, "Bethel Church will be like Ezekiel's river!"

I still was not sure what Ezekiel's river had to do with the Church, but as I prayed, I was getting rocked inside. I was eager to hang out with the Lord so that I could wrap my brain around the concept and get some understanding of what He and I were boldly declaring.

The Pool of Bethesda

As I sought the Lord, I began to realize that the Kingdom of God is experiencing one of the greatest transitions in human history. The Lord showed me that the pool of Bethesda represents, in parable or picture form, where we are as the Church today, and the river in the book of Ezekiel characterizes where we are going. To see the significance of this transition, let's begin by looking at the pool first:

> Now there is in Jerusalem by the sheep gate a pool, which is called in Hebrew Bethesda, having five porticoes. In these lay a multitude of those who were sick, blind, lame, and withered, [waiting for the moving of the waters; for an angel of the Lord went down at certain seasons into the pool and stirred up the water; whoever then first, after the stirring up of the water,

stepped in was made well from whatever disease with which he was afflicted.]

John 5:2–4

Did you notice that the pool of Bethesda had five porticoes? These kinds of details never used to mean much to me, until I realized a while ago the implication of the apostle John's statement "And there are also many other things which Jesus did, which if they were written in detail, I suppose that even the world itself would not contain the books that would be written" (John 1:25). Because God reduced the things that were written about Jesus down to just a few hundred pages, it stands to reason that every word He decided to include in His manuscript must be meaningful.

The details are also important because most of the gospels are eyewitness accounts. If a person witnessed an accident between two automobiles and happened to mention that both cars had hubcaps in recounting the story to a police officer, you would suspect that the hubcaps played some role in the accident. Otherwise, why would the person mention something so minor?

When the Lord first gave me the word about the Church being the pool of Bethesda, I was drawn to this description of the five porticoes surrounding the pool and began to consider their prophetic significance. Scripture indicates that these five porches provided covering for those who needed healing. The Lord revealed to me that this was a picture of the fivefold ministry (the apostle, prophet, evangelist, pastor and teacher). According to Ephesians 4:7–11, the fivefold ministers of Christ each have been commissioned to equip the saints for ministry. The five porticoes at the pool of Bethesda create an amazing picture of how these ministers, working together in unity, cover the Body of Christ, providing access to the raw power of God and the grace distributed by angels.

I came to understand that the fivefold ministry was transitioning by emerging out of obscurity and merging into the pool of unity. In other words, when the apostle, prophet, evangelist, pastor and teacher flow together and create a healthy governmental covering over the saints, this covering forms a kind of celestial vortex that creates strategic alliances with our heavenly allies. The implication of the word was that the Lord was establishing the fivefold ministry in His Church, and that the outcome would be increased angelic activity manifested by extraordinary miracles rarely witnessed in the history of the planet.

Two Governments

Since I had discovered the significance of the prophetic word about the pool, it was no wonder that the Lord's interruption in our prayer meeting that morning caught me off guard. Why would we need to move from this reality of unity, grace and power to something else? But as I began to search out this new word and compare the picture of the pool of Bethesda with the metaphor of the river in the book of Ezekiel, a new aspect and a deeper revelation of the pool began to unfold. The essence of this revelation is that, while the pool of Bethesda, with its five porticoes, does speak of the five ministry roles in Ephesians, it also represents a governmental structure that is fundamentally different from the organization represented by Ezekiel's river. The pool represents a *pastorate*, and the river represents an *apostleship*.

By now you are probably asking, "Kris, what are you talking about?" In order to explain these types of government, let me back up a little and explain what I mean by *government*. First, we need to understand that there is a difference between *government* and *governors*. I confused these terms for years. I used to preach that the fivefold ministry was the "government of God." Then one day I had a revelation that *government* is actually the *structure* in which governors, who are the officials, govern. I also came to understand that *leadership* is the *art of governing*. Through this revelation, I realized how important government is to governors. A governmental structure either empowers or constrains the ability of governors to lead effectively.

We can see the difference between government and governors by looking at our American government, which we call government by the people, for the people. When our forefathers drafted our Constitution, they were interested in creating a very different governmental structure from the British monarchy that once had ruled them. They thought Britain's king had way too much power. In response, they created a constitutional republic fashioned to limit our president's authority and balance the decision-making power among the branches of government and the majority of the citizens.

As our forefathers contemplated our young country's future, however, they realized that if our nation were ever under siege by an enemy on our own shores, a government with all these checks and balances would process decisions too slowly to win a war. With this in mind, they provided something in our Constitution called *martial law*. When Congress enacts martial law, it transforms our governmental structure from a constitutional republic to a military government, which empowers the role of the president above the other two branches.

Martial law means that our commander in chief can lead our troops without having to get the battle plan approved by the majority, thereby giving him or her the ability to make the quick decisions necessary to win a war. Unless martial law is enacted, the United States could have the greatest military general in history as its president, but the governmental structure itself would restrict his or her ability to lead our forces into victory in the event of a siege inside our borders. This is a great example of how a governmental structure can either empower or restrain its governors.

Designing Governmental Structures

For a long time, I have watched organizations build governmental structures around their leaders that hamstring their God-given abilities. Then later, the leaders are blamed for not performing well. It is crucial that we understand the three main factors that great governments must consider if they are going to be successful. (This is applicable in every organization, but our focus here is the Church.) First, who is leading? Second, who are the people they are leading? And third, in what epoch season are they leading these people? (Biblically speaking, an epoch season is a *way* in which God deals with a certain people in a certain time.) Misunderstanding any of these factors will cause the formation of governmental structures that limit, resist or even derail their people's God-given purposes.

Organizations could learn a great lesson from the contractor who built our community college in Redding, California. When Shasta College was constructed several years ago, the contractor did not install the sidewalks immediately after finishing the buildings. Instead, he planted lawns around the entire campus and took a year to observe where people wore out the grass. Then the contractor poured sidewalks in the worn sections of the lawn so that the walkways best facilitated the movement of the students and faculty to their destinations.

Government and its governmental structures are like those sidewalks. Such sidewalks are supposed to facilitate the gifts, passions and purposes of the God-given destinies of both the people who are leading and those being led, as well as the epoch season in which they are leading. But often, organizations construct governmental sidewalks with little or no regard for these factors. In so doing, they make it hard, if not impossible, for the people operating in these organizations to embrace their dreams and fulfill their destinies.

On the other hand, great organizations are developed when their leaders carefully analyze the three dynamics or factors I listed and then build governmental structures that best empower them. The outcome of this kind of formation is that it actually facilitates the organization's destiny instead of constraining it.

The Pool versus the River

With this in mind, let's look at the contrast between the pool of Bethesda and Ezekiel's river and see how the governmental structures they represent, the *pastorate* and the *apostleship*, relate to the three factors of government listed above (who is leading, whom they are leading and the epoch season they are in). The *pastorate* defines the three factors of government as follows: The leader is a pastor who is essentially a shepherd. Like a shepherd gathering his sheep, the pastor has a God-given anointing to gather people and tend to their needs. The people who follow the shepherd are obviously the sheep—people whose primary job is to stay together and stay healthy. Pastorates thrive when people perceive the season to be one in which these goals of staying together and staying healthy define their primary purpose.

The typical pastorate structure is seen clearly in the picture of the pool of Bethesda, where people *gathered* in order to have a supernatural encounter. And if they were going to have a supernatural encounter, they had to be there in the right season and they had to be the first person in the pool when the angel stirred the water. People come to most churches today for the same reason. If you want to be touched by God, you come to church. If you need to get saved, you come to church. If you need to be healed, counseled, taught or delivered, you come to church. You get the idea. The emphasis is on coming to church, and thus, the meetings are designed to meet the various needs of the Body. It also seems to me that what was true of the pool of Bethesda is generally true of pastorates—miracles happen in pastorates, but they are infrequent and inconsistent. There are seasonal visitations, but many people still lie along the edge of the pool and await their turn for an encounter.

Ezekiel's river provides us with a very different picture that represents an *apostleship*:

> Then he brought me back to the door of the house; and behold, water was flowing from under the threshold of the house toward the east, for the house faced east. And the water was flowing down from under, from the right side of the house, from south of the altar. He brought me out by way of the north gate and led me around on the outside to the outer gate by way of the gate that faces east. And behold, water was trickling from the south side.
>
> When the man went out toward the east with a line in his hand, he measured a thousand cubits, and he led me through the water, water reaching the ankles. Again he measured a thousand and led me through the water, water reaching the knees. Again he measured a thousand and led me through the water, water reaching the loins. Again he measured a thousand; and it was a river that I could not ford, for the water had risen, enough water to swim in, a river that could not be forded. He said to me, "Son of man, have you seen this?" Then he brought me back to the bank of the river. Now when I had returned, behold, on the bank of the river there were very many trees on the one side and on the other. Then he said to me, "These waters go out toward the eastern region and go

down into the Arabah; then they go toward the sea, being made to flow into the sea, and the waters of the sea become fresh. It will come about that every living creature which swarms in every place where the river goes, will live. And there will be very many fish, for these waters go there and the others become fresh; so everything will live where the river goes. And it will come about that fishermen will stand beside it; from Engedi to Eneglaim there will be a place for the spreading of nets. Their fish will be according to their kinds, like the fish of the Great Sea, very many. But its swamps and marshes will not become fresh; they will be left for salt. By the river on its bank, on one side and on the other, will grow all kinds of trees for food. Their leaves will not wither and their fruit will not fail. They will bear every month because their water flows from the sanctuary, and their fruit will be for food and their leaves for healing."

Ezekiel 47:1–12

We can gather a lot of revelation from this vision. Notice that this river, which (like the water in the pool) represents the grace of God, flows out from under the sanctuary door and becomes deeper the farther it gets from the sanctuary. This depicts a *movement* in which God's presence grows more powerful as the *people of God* take His presence into the world with them into businesses, homes, schools and so forth. Also notice that the farther the saints get from the sanctuary, the deeper the grace of God penetrates the darkness. In other words, the greatest miracles, the most powerful expressions of the Kingdom, are destined to happen in the worst places on the planet, not inside the walls of a building.

Sent Ones

In the pastorate model the needy come to a central location, the pool, to get healed. In the apostolic model the river flows through our cities, and everyone it touches gets healed and becomes fresh. Pastors *gather*, like the pool, but apostles *send*, like the river.

This river metaphor fits an apostleship so well because the word *apostle* comes from the secular Roman world, and it means "sent one." Roman "apostles" were not only sent; they had a very specific purpose. The Romans were aggressive about expanding their empire, and they wisely employed Alexander the Great's strategy in doing so. He established the Greek Empire by conquering kingdoms and then culturizing them in the Greek ways. Without establishing Greek culture, these conquered peoples would not have assimilated into their new national identity and government. Likewise, the Romans developed envoys to culturize their conquered cities in the ways of Rome. (This is where we get the old adage "When in Rome, do as the Romans do.") Roman generals called *apostles* most often led these envoys, with the commission that they bring Roman civilization into these new territories. They were to transform the legal, financial, educational and all other systems so that the new land would seem like home even to the emperor himself, should he decide to visit there. Through the labor of the Roman apostles, new territories became desirable outposts of Rome.

It is interesting that when Jesus promoted His disciples from learners to leaders, He did not call them *patriarchs*. They would have had some idea of how patriarchs led, as an Old Testament model for those was already in place. Neither did He call them *priests*, *prophets* or *rabbis*, because again there were patterns of order already developed for those roles. Instead, He called them by a Roman title that would forever define their ministry responsibility and authority. Like the Roman armies that first battled for territory and then educated the conquered people in the Roman ways, the apostles of Jesus were commissioned to displace the powers of darkness with the power of God and replace the enemy's authority with the government of God, bringing the influence of the Kingdom's ways into every aspect of society.

We see the mission of apostles expressed in the only "model" prayer Jesus taught His leaders. Jesus said, "Pray, then, in this way: 'Our Father who is in heaven, hallowed be Your name. Your kingdom come. Your will be done, on earth as it is in heaven'" (Matthew 6:9–10). The emphasis in the Lord's Prayer is that earth would become like heaven. In the same way that the Romans were to make their conquered cities look like Rome, we have been commissioned to pull heaven down to earth, until the will of God is done here exactly as it is there. Apostleships thrive in a season when people perceive that their primary purpose is to transform the culture of earth with the culture of heaven.

Making the Transition

In late 2007, the Lord spoke to me and said, *Mankind has just entered into the new apostolic age. Yet the modern world has never experienced the true power of an apostle, because apostles have emerged in a pastorate form of government that restricts, constrains and often usurps their ability to govern.*

For the most part, the Church has only empowered apostles to plant churches. But apostles were never meant merely to be church planters: they were called to be world changers! A leader can plant one hundred churches in different cities around the world, but if those churches don't bring cultural transformation to their cities, then they are not apostolic. Cultural transformation is synonymous with apostolic ministry.

Think about it. If we gather five thousand people week after week on Sunday mornings in a city of half a million, yet the crime rate remains unchanged, the cancer rate is unaffected, the divorce rate continues to grow and the economy is in decline, what does that say about the people of God in that city?

If we are supposed to be salt and light, and all the nations of the earth are to be blessed in us, then isn't it true that the negative statistics of our cities are a commentary on us? Look at the commentary on the first-century Church in Acts 17. The Jews cried out to the rulers of the city, "These who have turned the world upside down have come here too" (verse 6 NKJV). What does it say about us if we cannot even change one city with thousands of believers? The truth is, a pastorate form of government is not designed to transform cities. It is developed to attract people and create a culture where flocks gather to get healthy and happy. Pastorates are, to some degree, irrelevant to their city's culture because their churches' governmental structures are built to congregate, not to deploy.

This principle is evident when you look at American cities statistically. Demographically, the cities that have the greatest Christian churchgoing population density also have some of the worst social statistics in our country (with the exception of a few cities). In other words, the cities that have the highest crime rates, the most divorces, the greatest number of abortions per capita, the highest levels of poverty and the poorest health statistics also have the best church attendance. What we need to understand is that gathering believers for two hours on a Sunday morning is *not* synonymous with cultural transformation. Pastorates simply are culturally ineffective by design.

Apostleships, on the other hand, are developed around the principle of training, equipping and deploying the saints to radically alter society. The primary message of apostleships is that the Kingdom of God is at hand, and their main strategy is to demonstrate the raw power of God in the darkest places on the planet. The apostolic government, like Ezekiel's river, creates a supernatural atmosphere that affects everything it touches, from the fish (people) in the river to the trees (nations and cities) along its banks. Wherever the river flows, things get healed, become fresh and are supernaturally productive (producing fruit every month instead of one season a year). This river is the perfect metaphor for the emerging apostolic age.

That is not to say that there is no place for pastors. But the key to making pastorates effective is that *apostleships must empower pastorates*. Obviously, in order to deploy people into the darkest places of the planet, the saints need to be gathered and be healthy and happy. It is impossible for us to create a culture around us that we don't have within us. It is therefore essential that apostleships build and empower pastorates within them that develop happy and healthy sheep. In fact, depending on the size of an apostle's *metron* (Greek for "measure"), an apostleship may include many pastorates under its covering.

The transition from a pastorate model to an apostolic form of church government does not eliminate the pastorate, but repositions it within the greater purpose of the apostolic mission. This epoch season change is one in which God is still emphasizing *gathering*, but in the context of *deployment*. Pastorates still will gather the sheep, but they will not seek to get them healthy and happy simply as an end in itself, but as preparation for them being sent out to change the world.

Working in Harmony

It is paramount that the fivefold governors merge in a way that facilitates their proper places in Christ and empowers them to operate in their God-given roles. This will result in the Body being equipped with the grace to build *itself* up in love as it accomplishes the Great Commission to make disciples of all nations.

As the Church makes this transition from one governmental model to another, meetings like Sunday morning services will be transformed from social gatherings into Holy Spirit super-natural training sessions. Our services will continue to embrace worship, fellowship, healing, prophecy, teaching and so on, but with the apostolic purpose of cultural reformation at their core.

The book of Isaiah provides a great example of the fruit of pastoral ministry and apostolic mission flowing together. First, Isaiah the prophet pronounces the restoration of individual people in every dimension of their lives:

> The Spirit of the Lord GOD is upon me, because the LORD has anointed me to bring good news to the afflicted; He has sent me to bind up the brokenhearted, to proclaim liberty to captives and freedom to prisoners; to proclaim the favorable year of the LORD and the day of vengeance of our God; to comfort all who mourn, to grant those who mourn in Zion, giving them a garland instead of ashes, the oil of gladness instead of mourn-ing, the mantle of praise instead of a spirit of fainting. So they will be called oaks of righteousness, the planting of the LORD, that He may be glorified.
>
> Isaiah 61:1–3

Then Isaiah goes on to prophesy that these same people who experienced personal transformation will be commissioned to rebuild their cities:

> Then they will rebuild the ancient ruins, they will raise up the former devastations; and they will repair the ruined cities, the desolations of many generations.
>
> Isaiah 61:4

This is a great example of the teamwork that is to take place between apostles and pastors, resulting in happy and healthy people having a dynamic, positive impact on their cities. We need the entire fivefold ministry working in harmony together like a beautiful orchestra, with the apostle being the conductor.

The Bethel Story

When Bill and Beni Johnson became the senior leaders of Bethel Church in 1996, the church was definitely a pastorate. The Johnsons replaced Ray Larson, a true fivefold pastor with a real passion for the lost. It was a lampstand church, and under Larson's leadership, the fellowship had become a great place for people to get saved and discipled. He and his leadership team had done a great job of growing the church from a few hundred people to a congregation of nearly two thousand over a period of eight years. They developed leaders for church ministry, emphasized connections in social gatherings, formed sports teams, produced large Christmas and Easter performances, held community events and established Christian schools, to name just a few things they did. People felt connected and taken care of.

When Kathy and I joined Bill and Beni in 1998, the church was already in the midst of a very quick transition from a pastorate to an apostleship. Bill is an amazing apostle with a mandate to reform the Church, and I am a prophet with a passion for cultural transformation. Under this new mission, Bethel became a catalyst for a movement focused on the core values of the goodness of God and the supernatural power of the Spirit. But what became evident behind the scenes was that we had a desperate need for a pastorate within our movement. It was not that we did not have pastors on staff. We did. We actually had eight pastors on our team. What we lacked was the structure that facilitated their strength, valued their ministry approach and empowered their need for a greater relational context in our church.

What we discovered in that season at Bethel Church was that pastors need a pastorate form of government to be successful, but that most of them cannot build the structure themselves. It takes a special pastor/builder to pour the necessary sidewalks, so to speak, that ensure that they reach the destiny of their office and calling. Another important component necessary to empower pastors successfully is that apostles and prophets need to be sensitive to the pastoral perspective and worldview. The very virtue of the pastoral calling causes them to have a dramatically different approach to life.

Apostolic and prophetic core values can sometimes seem to undermine the values that reinforce pastoral care. For example, apostles and prophets by nature tend to emphasize miracles, healings and other supernatural interventions of God. Apostleships tend to highlight the instant, immediate and spontaneous. The side effect of this perspective is that the prolonged pastoral processes of restoration common in counseling, discipleship and caring for the chronically ill who have yet to experience healing can seem devalued. True fivefold pastors work best in a highly relational environment where they can love people into wholeness over time.

Bill and I began to realize that we needed someone who could build highways that empowered our pastoral ministry. With this in mind, in 2001 we brought Danny and Sheri Silk to our team to develop a pastorate structure. Over the next five years, they assembled and empowered a pastoral team that nurtured our people into health. Danny started our Transformation Center, which incorporates more than fifty anointed people whom he trained in the counseling and deliverance ministry. Next, he built the Pastor On Call ministry for people who could not wait for an appointment because of emergency situations. Under Danny's guidance, volunteers now staff most of this ministry. He also empowered a team that ministers to those waiting for healing. Danny and Sheri are a great example of gifted pastors who can replicate themselves and who know how to build pastorate governmental structures.

Bethel's New Epoch Season

In 2006 the Lord once again took Bethel Church to another level in the Kingdom. He gave us a word that drastically altered our governmental structure again. He said, *You have a church that has a movement, but the movement has outgrown the church. Consequently, your governmental structure, which was built for a previous season, is inadequate to lead in this epoch season. I want you to develop a governmental structure for a movement that has a church.*

This prophetic word became a catalyst of a five-year transition that culminated in a radically different structure at Bethel Church. We divided our apostleship into four separate divisions: the local church, the movement, the school of ministry and our businesses. In 2011 Candace and Eric Johnson became the senior leaders of our local church. They are both pastors (although Eric also has a strong apostolic call on his life). We commissioned them to shepherd and oversee all aspects of Bethel Church. They immediately developed a new core team of leaders to shepherd the church and care for our people. At the same time, we developed another team to oversee our responsibility to influence and disciple nations. The ministry school already had its own core leadership team, as did our business team.

The results have been amazing. Our church has grown exponentially both spiritually and numerically. *Community* is Bethel Church's new buzzword, as Candace and Eric infuse our culture with a new sense of belonging. Our people have about fifty proactive places they can plug in to serve and become connected.

The impact, depth and reach of our movement have also grown significantly. We are reaching world leaders in nearly every sphere of society. We can see nations being discipled in the near future. Hope is rising in our hearts as Jesus is beginning to open some of the most amazing doors to us.

The Right Ingredients

We are learning firsthand that all of the fivefold ministers need governmental structures that empower their strengths and cover their weaknesses. We have only concentrated on two of them in this chapter, apostles and pastors. But without government that is specifically developed for prophets, teachers and evangelists, these ministers also will be largely ineffective.

One of the symptoms of governmental dysfunction is the overemphasis or underemphasis on a particular office. For example, if the pastoral ministry has "freeways" to run on and the prophetic ministry has only "rugged trails" to traverse, safety will be overemphasized and adventure and risk will be underemphasized. Pastors work to create safe places for people to grow up in. They love predictable environments that don't scare the flock. But this can lead them to downplay other elements of Christ's nature. We need to remember that the same Jesus who made sinners feel at home with Him also overturned tables, drove money changers out of the Temple with a whip, called a woman a dog and ostracized the religious leaders of His day.

If there is insufficient evangelistic grace flowing into the congregational pool, the church will stagnate with old growth. Consequently, succession planning will be virtually nonexistent because there will be no new believers to carry the mission into the next generation. If the evangelistic ministry is overstated (which is impossible, according to most evangelists), then a church, metaphorically speaking, will be a huge nursery with nobody in it qualified to care for the infants.

When a church lacks the adequate influence of true fivefold teachers, biblical foundations give way to subjective experiences and feelings. But when the teacher's role is overemphasized, Christians typically will become overinformed and underexperienced.

It takes all of the fivefold offices—apostles, prophets, evangelists, pastors and teachers—to equip a fully functioning Body. Every baker knows that it does not simply take the right ingredients to make a great cookie; it takes the right amount of each ingredient. Good government empowers the entire fivefold ministry proportionally, so that there is the right amount of each ingredient (office) in the Body of Christ.

6

∷∷∷∷∷∷∷∷∷∷∷∷∷∷∷∷∷∷∷∷∷∷∷

Ecosystems

With the demise of the biblical religions that have provided the American people with their core values since
their country's inception, we are reverting to the pagan
worldview. Trees and animals are venerated, while man is
simply one more animal in the ecosystem—and largely a
hindrance, not an asset.

Dennis Prager

I sat in our claw-foot bathtub, enjoying the hot water that
enveloped my tired body. The longer I soaked, the cooler
the water became, until I finally had to either get out or add
more hot water to the tub. As I contemplated my cool situation,
I realized that the water in the tub would eventually become
room temperature, not one degree hotter or colder. The room
had an ecosystem that maintained the climate, while the bathtub had no such ecosystem; therefore, 70 degrees would be the

prevailing temperature of everything in the room. I came to realize that 70 degrees is not in itself a dominant temperature, but what made it dominant was the ecosystem in the room, which in this case was the heating and air-conditioning system.

In other words, *what we cultivate dominates*. I started to think about how my simple experience applied to the mindset of a city, or to the belief system of a nation. I was stunned by the thought that the morality of a nation is determined by the prevailing ecosystem, not the dominance of the virtue itself. Good only triumphs over evil if good has a more dominant ecosystem. On the other hand, if evil has an ecosystem and good has none, evil will prevail every time.

I also started to think about the mindset shift that has taken place in America during my lifetime. For example, in my grandfather's day homosexuality was practiced by a few, but society in general was appalled by it. It was listed as a mental disorder and treated by psychotherapists. But in fifty short years, our society has embraced homosexuality as a normal sexual orientation protected by our laws and taught to children in our public schools. In fact, in 2015 America passed laws legalizing same-sex marriage.

Did America finally get it right? Is homosexuality normal, or is it just common? (Remember, cancer is common, but it will never be normal.) Did the mindset of our nation shift because embracing homosexuality is the right thing to do? No! *Good* and *evil* do not in themselves have the ability to prevail; it is the ecosystem that determines what prevails in the hearts of people and in the mindsets of nations.

Creating Ecosystems

A thermostat adjusts my bedroom's ecosystem, and a complex heating and air-conditioning system maintains it. The A/C system was specifically designed by taking into account several factors like the size of the room, the percentage of window to wall space, the height of the ceilings and the climate of the area we live in. Remember, the ecosystem in my bedroom is working inside of a larger ecosystem called Mother Nature. My A/C system is not powerful enough to maintain a certain temperature inside my entire yard; it needs the walls of the house to insulate the bedroom from the exterior climate. The walls and roof of my house are therefore an important part of the ecosystem.

You may be asking, "Okay, Kris, where are you going with all this?" I simply am trying to point out that in the same way that a room's climate is controlled by the most dominant ecosystem, the culture of cities or nations is also determined by the prevailing ecosystems that are perpetuated by and for its citizens.

Ecosystems influence mindsets, which ultimately produce cultures, which determine the way people live, love and think. Ecosystems are produced inactively, reactively and proactively. When people stumble through life with no motivation, no vision and no purpose, their inactivity actually creates a negative ecosystem that perpetuates a welfare mentality, which holds them in the bondage of a poverty culture.

Inactive ecosystems are the result of people living out of unconscious ignorance. They have no idea how their life affects or is affected by the world around them; therefore, life just happens to them and through them. I call these people the "row, row, row your boat gently down the stream" people. They often feel powerless, overwhelmed and directionless. They are victims of the streams of life, with no rudder or oars to guide them. And when the gentle streams of life turn into raging rivers, they usually find themselves either crashing on the rocks of offense or staggering over the stones of stumbling.

Reactive ecosystems are created and perpetuated by people who were abused or negatively affected by some person or circumstance in their life. These people react by doing the opposite of their abusers. It can be as simple as the dynamics that play out in a family between a permissive mother and an overly strict father. The mother reacts to the father's strict discipline by refusing to set any boundaries or provide any discipline for the children. The father's harsh discipline and the mother's unsanctified mercy create and perpetuate an ecosystem that ultimately manifests in the way their children are raised. The children usually play upon the adversarial relationship between their parents, and their response becomes another important part of the ecosystem. All of these reactions result in an unhealthy and dysfunctional culture.

Proactive ecosystems are created when influencers design a desired culture and then proactively begin to build an ecosystem that produces and perpetuates that culture. Let's see if we can envision the steps necessary to develop a proactive ecosystem:

1. Every social ecosystem begins in the hearts and minds of people and spreads through a complex system of communication. Ecosystems are fortified through belief systems that affect the way we think, the way we view life and the way we process our relationships with people.

2. Belief systems become core values that have agreed-upon behaviors. For example, maybe you believe that you should love your neighbor as you love yourself. In order for this belief to become an ecosystem, it must be tied to a behavior. In other words, what does loving your neighbor look like?

3. Your belief system is like adjusting your bedroom's thermostat to 70 degrees in the summer. The cool air blowing out of the A/C vents represents the behaviors that manifest from your convictions.

4. Ecosystems begin to take shape when people consistently live out their beliefs in their behaviors, despite resistance

from the ignorant, conflict with adversaries and the struggle with the environment.

5. The number of influential people who assimilate a similar belief system and then act out their core beliefs in their daily lives will determine the level of influence their ecosystem has on society.

6. When enough people embrace a particular system of belief and live its principles out in their lives, an ecosystem develops. When this ecosystem is lived out long enough, it creates a culture.

7. Core values (beliefs) often remain consistent in an ecosystem, while cultures tend to be in a constant state of metamorphosis as people find (or are forced into) new expressions of the same core values. For example, let's say that you believe your family should come first. When your children are infants, you therefore get up in the middle of the night to feed and care for them. But this same core value is manifested differently when they become teenagers. The ecosystem must evolve to embrace the same core values, with the same "family first" outcomes. Although the desired outcome is still "family first," the shift in ecosystems necessary to meet this demand in a way that is relevant to teenagers will necessitate a shift in culture. In other words, you may get up four times a night to walk out your "family first" values when you have infants. But you might become a soccer mom/taxi driver when those same kids become teenagers.

8. Cultures are the manifestation of beliefs that are lived out systematically, until they create their own ecosystem that produces the desired outcomes in the intended environment.

At this point you might be asking, "What's the difference between cultures and ecosystems?" That is a great question.

Let me explain it like this: I have a 2013 Dodge truck that has 485 horsepower, air-conditioning and Sirius radio. This year my wife, Kathy, bought me a new Corvette for our fortieth wedding anniversary. My Corvette also has 485 horsepower, air-conditioning and Sirius radio. Yet the driving experience in the car is completely different than the driving experience in the truck.

Both vehicles share many common core values, so to speak, and thus have similar ecosystems. The ecosystems are the engine, chassis, brake system, air-conditioning, lighting and so forth. Yet each vehicle was designed with specific outcomes in mind. The truck has an eight-foot bed in which to carry cargo, because it was designed to haul heavy loads. The Corvette has only two seats, which makes it lighter, because it was designed to go fast.

If the vehicle components are the ecosystems, the experience I have when I am driving each vehicle is the culture. In other words, cultures are created through a *coalition* of ecosystems that are assembled to perpetuate a *desired* experience.

Thermometer or Thermostat?

The question is, are you a thermometer or a thermostat? Are you the person who is affected by the culture around you, or are you the person who is helping create that culture? Many people go through life feeling like powerless victims of their environment. They are thermometers. They reflect the culture around them because the culture happens to them, but they are unaware of it or are unwilling to influence it.

Becoming a culture catalyst—a thermostat—requires that you gain influence by being valued by the gatekeepers of the environment. You only have as much influence in people's lives as they place value on you (an idea we will come back to in the next chapter). You must find something that the gatekeepers need and get good at providing it. Or maybe you have a great gift in some area of your life and you can figure out a way to use it to gain value.

This is the way Joseph and Daniel gained influence in their perspective countries, as we talk about more in some other chapters. They both had the ability to interpret dreams, and Daniel was also incredibly wise. Their supernatural abilities gave them an audience with kings, which ultimately provided a platform from which they could adjust the thermostat of their nations.

Solomon put it like this: "A man's gift makes room for him and brings him before great men" (Proverbs 18:16). Joseph and Daniel were thermostats, not thermometers. Rather than being influenced by the culture around them, they helped create culture.

The Redding Story

We live and work in a Northern California city called Redding. It is a city of about ninety thousand people that was established in the late 1800s as a timber and mining community. In the last fifty years mining has virtually disappeared, while the lumber industry in Redding is a shadow of its former glory. You can probably guess that this has adversely affected our city in a number of ways. Julie Winter captured our situation beautifully in her campaign speech for Redding City Council. She said,

> We find ourselves in the midst of what might be the greatest transition in the history of our city. This transition strikes at the very heart of who we are, both as a people, and as a community. Just fifty short years ago, our city was buzzing with activity; logging trucks lined our roads, loaded with trees full of money. The sound of whirling saws echoed from our mills from twilight

until dawn, filling the air with prosperity for our families. Our restaurants, pubs, shops and markets were alive with loggers' tales, whispered and wondered . . . told around tables . . . beautiful stories, fresh from the forest. Renewable revenue flowed with abundance to our police, firemen and schools. Jobs were plentiful and the unemployed were few . . . wages were high, and the provision was abundant.

It's actually true that our money used to grow on trees, but no longer. . . . Gone are most of the rugged men in their tattered jeans and flannel shirts. Gone are many of the trucks carrying trees, and the heavy equipment operators. Gone are the multitude of chain saws, truck shops and tractor repairs. Gone are most of the whirling saws, lumber mills and massive cranes. Gone are most of the choppers carrying logs, the water trucks and the crew rigs. And with them our way of life has slowly digressed . . . as the splendor of a former season faded into obscurity.

But a new day is longing to emerge from the sawdust of yesterday's prosperity in Redding. It's a pilgrimage of unprecedented expansion. And much like those rugged families who forged a way of life through the wilderness, we are pioneers in a different kind of wilderness . . . a wilderness of social transition, economic redefinition and divine providence. Therefore, it is incumbent upon us as citizens of this beautiful city to rediscover our purpose, clarify our plans and redefine our destiny.

In the fourteenth century, Europe experienced a cultural rebirth, which yielded a 300-year Renaissance. This Renaissance wasn't predicated on an economic collapse. Instead, it emerged from the catacombs of historic literature and art, as well as the awaking of the scientific age. Italian cities like Florence and Milan became catalysts of creativity. Much like Hollywood, New York, Nashville and Silicon Valley, these cities became melting pots for discovery . . . places where visionaries gathered to collaborate and create.

Could Redding be the next city of opportunity? . . . Is it possible that the beauty surrounding us is more than a tourist attraction? . . . Could the splendor around us awaken the creativity within us, to flow through us, to inspire another Renaissance from us?

Think about this: Our community was once filled with miners in search of hidden treasures dredged from our waters and sifted from our soil. Yet the most valuable commodity of our generation is not gold, silver or even diamonds; it is ideas . . . that's right . . . intellectual properties top the commodity list! More people in the Information Age invest in inventions, innovations and revelation than in all the other commodities combined.

I believe that this city is standing at the dawn of creativity, a place where ingenuity isn't just inspired, but is actually quarried from the minds of people. I would like to propose to you that Redding could be the next Florence of Italy, or the next Geneva of Switzerland . . . a place where visionaries collaborate, and artists, inventors, innovators, scientists, writers, entrepreneurs, actors, dancers, singers and musicians (just to name a few) gather to see their dreams realized.

In the same way that the Sacramento River runs through our city, both giving life to its citizens and carrying hope to millions of others who have access to its streams, Redding could become a source of inspiration for both its people and for the nations.

Reformers Arise

Julie Winter is a reformer who is destined to become a thermostat that changes the climate of our city. She is part of our strategic leadership team whose members long to see our city prosper and become a light to the nations. In 2008, our leadership team was contemplating our city's situation and asking the hard questions. The front page of our local newspaper had just carried the annual report that ranks cities in the order of their quality of life. Redding was again ranked among the worst cities in America to live in. We dialogued for a long time about how disheartening it was to be a church of eight thousand people in a city of ninety thousand, and yet to realize that our own prosperous church culture was having little effect on the social statistics of our city. We asked ourselves what we could do as a church to begin to transform Redding.

The recession had taken a huge toll on our city. Redding desperately needed money to meet the basic needs of our community. Fire protection, police protection and education were significantly underfunded. We knew we could not solve the problem by ourselves, but we had to do what we could. We decided to give 10 percent of our people's tithe to our city every month.

We made an appointment with our city manager and explained our intentions to him in detail. He asked us how we wanted the money spent. We told him that the people in the early Church who wanted to help their community had given their money directly to their leaders and had let them decide how to disperse it. We wanted to follow the same principle so that we could both build trust and meet the pressing needs of our community.

We asked our city manager for two things in return: First, we did not want him to make any press releases about our giving. Second, we asked that he meet with us once a year to keep us apprised of the specific needs in our city. We told him that we also were going to take offerings for specific projects throughout the year. It was a beautiful moment in our history. Bill and I left the city manager's office knowing that something profound and powerful had just taken place.

Motives Are Everything

We wanted to make it clear that we were not trying to buy influence or force our agenda on anyone. The truth is, we had no agenda. In fact, we did not even have a plan to help our city at that time, outside of contributing some money. I am not sure what our city manager thought about our presentation, but he seemed a little skeptical. After all, Christians are famous for trying to force their will on their communities, so I don't blame him if he did not trust us at first.

Time passed while our leadership team continued to collaborate and dream together. We have a full-time ministry school with two thousand students enrolled. We were teaching our students about cultural transformation, so it just made sense that we should give them some practical experience by putting them to work on our city. We went back to our city manager and shared our plan with him and his team. We told them that we wanted to put two thousand students to work doing whatever it took to help make Redding amazing.

I could tell that our city leaders did not quite catch the vision at first, but at least they were willing to assign us some trivial tasks. We were excited to prove ourselves to them, yet unfortunately it took a while before we got it right. We did not realize how much organization it would take to put a couple thousand students to work doing anything meaningful. We failed miserably the first year. We had our outreach team overseeing our city assignments. Fifty students would descend on a park with one rake and two brooms. Consequently, three people would be working, while forty-seven people watched. Furthermore, our instructions from the city were so vague that we were never really sure what we were supposed to do. Also, when the weather was bad our teams did nothing at all. We were discouraged, but we were not ready to give up yet.

Our leadership team continued to dialogue for several months, until we finally decided that if we were really going to transform our city, we were going to have to make a significantly deeper commitment. We scraped together enough money to hire an excellent project supervisor named Keith Alvord. We shared the vision with him and asked Keith to put together a plan that would rock our city. Nearly another year passed as Keith built a management structure, bought $200,000 worth of equipment and built trust with our city leaders. By the third year we were making some excellent progress. We asked our students to do their menial city assignments the way Solomon's servants waited on tables. We read the following passages to them and challenged them to make history by doing ordinary tasks in extraordinary ways.

> Now when the queen of Sheba heard about the fame of Solomon concerning the name of the LORD, she came to test him with difficult questions. . . . When the queen of Sheba perceived all the wisdom of Solomon, the house that he had built, the food of his table, the seating of his servants, the attendance of his waiters and their attire, his cupbearers, and his stairway by which he went up to the house of the LORD, there was no more spirit in her. Then she said to the king, "It was a true report which I heard in my own land about your words and your wisdom. Nevertheless I did not believe the reports, until I came and my eyes had seen it. And behold, the half was not told me. You exceed in wisdom and prosperity the report, which I heard."
>
> 1 Kings 10:1, 4–7

The results were absolutely stunning. Our ministry students were sweeping streets and cleaning parks like Michelangelo chipped rock to free angels from stone!

A couple of years later, the city commissioned us to build a park in the middle of a huge blackberry patch by the river. Several other organizations had been working on it for ten years. Keith assembled a small army of students, and they descended on the plot of land like soldiers swarming onto a battlefield. Six months later, the dust cleared and the park was finished. Our local newspaper and TV stations followed the project, reporting on it often. Our teams began winning awards for their work. Soon our city was assigning us greater responsibility and more meaningful projects.

Bethel Saves the Convention Center

Redding was becoming a nicer place to live, but financial woes continued to plague our community. Finally, out of desperation, the Redding City Council decided to close our Redding Convention Center. It was costing the city of Redding $1.8 million a year just to keep the doors open. After closing a fire station and laying off several more police officers, our city council felt like there was no other choice but to close that building down.

In the meanwhile (a couple of years before all this happened), the Lord had been speaking to our Bethel Church team about taking over the convention center. A couple of our leaders had dreams about Bethel relocating our ministry there. In fact, I had actually approached the city manager about the possibility of Bethel buying the building, an idea in which they had no interest. Our leadership team began brainstorming around the idea of taking over the convention center and running it as a service to our community. The plan was to start a nonreligious, nonprofit public benefit corporation called Advance Redding, and use it to run the center as a secular venue. We would relocate our first-year ministry school there during the day and continue the secular entertainment in the center in the evenings and on weekends.

The ministry school would pay $750,000 annually for rent to Advance Redding, so that the financial plan would work. In addition, Advance Redding would pay $25,000 per month for rent to the city, to help with the city's financial crisis. Not only would Redding save $1.8 million with our plan, but also the city would gain $300,000 rent per year.

We knew we were taking a huge risk, but we really felt as though God was in it. We presented our plan to the city manager, who had become our friend. He and his team thought it was a beautiful plan. But a coalition of citizens in our community were afraid that we would turn the Redding Convention Center into a church, and eventually our city would look like Mormon Utah. They caught the attention of the media and stirred up quite a few people against us.

The day came to present our plan to the Redding City Council in a public forum. We asked our church members not to come to the meeting, because we were concerned that the mere size of our crowd would intimidate the city council members into passing our proposal. We wanted the council to accept our proposal because they thought it was the right thing to do for our city. Consequently, Charlie Harper, Julie Winter, April LaFrance and I arrived at City Hall as Bethel's representatives a few minutes before the meeting started. To our surprise, the place was packed with people from the opposition. They were carrying picket signs, and they had even hired several cheerleaders to lead the crowd in chanting against us.

The city council allowed each of the people who opposed our plan three minutes to present his or her argument and share an alternative plan. The council had asked our Advance Redding team to present our plan last. The tension in the room was so thick that you could cut it with a knife. The rowdy crowd cheered each time one of their people finished a presentation. Although the council pressed them, not one of the opposition had come up with an alternate plan. Finally, after 25 or so people had finished their obnoxious presentations, it was our turn. The council gave us 15 minutes to make our case. At first the crowd booed us and sneered, but as we continued our presentation the people went silent.

The three of us took five minutes to present our mission and vision statement for the Redding Convention Center, and then we used the next ten minutes to lay out our strategic plan. We had spent three months poring over the profit and loss statements for the building and studying the current business plan, so we were confident that we knew what we were talking about.

When we finished the last PowerPoint slide, the city council deliberated while the crowd listened in silence.

Twenty minutes later, the Redding City Council finally voted 4-1 to accept our proposal. The crowd was furious, and now we faced the tough task of showing that we could make it all work.

Climb or Die

We wanted to run the Redding Convention Center the same way our students beautified our city. Our goal was to make it an excellent experience for everyone who came into the building. We spent $500,000 remodeling the building and installing a state-of-the-art ticket system. We replaced all the seats, installed a new sound system and remodeled the entire interior of the building. We hired an almost entirely new staff, employing only friendly people who had a heart for excellence.

It took us two long years to learn the entertainment business, but we were passionate about getting it right. At first we lost money on many of the shows. To make matters worse, in our zeal to make sure the venue stayed secular and not "Christian," we booked some acts that were pure filth . . . actually nearly porn. At times things were tough, but we knew we had to climb or die.

For the first two years, the community (led by the media) scrutinized everything we did and cut us no slack. But as time went on, their fear of a "religious takeover" evaporated in light of the obviously improved experience our community was having in the convention center. We were hosting as many shows and events as ever, while still meeting the needs of our school there.

In our third year of managing the building, we finally began to win the praise of our community. In fact, many of the people who had protested against us that night at the city council meeting came back and apologized to our team. And our city manager and his team have since said openly, "This is the best the convention center has been run in 43 years!"

How About Your City?

Ask yourself if you are a thermometer or a thermostat in your city. Ask yourself if you are part of the ecosystem of heaven, or if your heart has become the temperature of the city around you.

Jesus rebuked the wealthy and yet ineffective church of Laodicea. He said, "I know your deeds, that you are neither cold nor hot; I wish that you were cold or hot. So because you are lukewarm, and neither hot nor cold, I will spit you out of My mouth" (Revelation 3:15–16).

It takes effort and energy to be hot or cold, but lukewarm is the temperature of the room. Lukewarm is the proverbial "thermometer life," born from a heart that reflects the culture around it but makes no effort to transform that culture.

The truth is, you cannot conquer what you refuse to confront. I want to challenge you to become a catalyst for a Kingdom ecosystem. Jesus fed five thousand people with a little boy's lunch. You would be surprised what Jesus can do with your life when you give it completely to Him.

7

::::::::::::::::::::::::::::::::::

"Mr. Gorbachev, Tear Down This Wall!"

Great spirits have always found violent opposition from mediocrities. The latter cannot understand it when a man does not thoughtlessly submit to hereditary prejudices, but honestly and courageously uses his intelligence.

Albert Einstein

If we really are in a new epoch season where God is leading us out of the stale bread of denominationalism into the fresh manna of apostleships, and if the main manifestation of apostleships is cultural transformation, then we must ask ourselves, how do we practically bring the Kingdom's influence to bear on this ailing planet? Is there a way to expose 7.4 billion people to our amazing King and make a way for His superior Kingdom to revolutionize the world's mindsets?

Jesus said, "Behold, I send you out as sheep in the midst of wolves; so be shrewd as serpents and innocent as doves" (Matthew 10:16). He also said, "The sons of this age are more shrewd in relation to their own kind than the sons of light" (Luke 16:8). It is time for us to study the tactics of serpents and the sons of this age so that we can emulate their strategies and overcome their purposes.

An Empire Crumbles

Let me give you a few examples of worldly tactics that have greatly influenced the course of history, and let me contrast them with the Church's approach to see if we can gain some valuable insights. I started the first grade in 1961, at the height of the Cold War. I have vivid memories of our elementary school teachers instructing us about how to respond in the case of a Russian attack. Eight hundred kids, their little hearts pounding out of their chests, would practice scrambling for "safety" under their small desks as the air raid alarm screamed over the PA system. I still remember lying awake at night as a young boy, envisioning warplanes flying over our house and dropping bombs on our neighborhood. I would pull the covers over my head, trembling at the thoughts that were pressed into my young mind.

My uncle Joe, who lived a couple of miles away from us, spent two years and thousands of dollars turning his backyard into an underground bomb shelter. I can still recall my parents having conversations with us about meeting them in my uncle's bomb shelter in the case of an air raid. Radio stations would practice their emergency broadcast system alerts about once a month. Of course, they would tell you before and after the alert, "This is just a test of the emergency broadcast system." Boy, if you happened to turn the radio on in the middle of one of those tests, you had to wait for what seemed like an eternity to find out if your neighborhood was under attack.

Those were times of uncertainty, high anxiety and extreme apprehension. But something happened between those early years of grade school and 1989. Without a shot fired or a bomb dropped, the Iron Curtain disintegrated. It really had little to do with the threat of the American military. Instead, this was an inside job. President Reagan had called on Russian president Mikhail Gorbachev to tear down the literal wall that separated East Germany and West Germany and the greater "wall" between Communist nations and the rest of the world.

That is exactly what happened. The people in those nations tore down the wall of Communism all by themselves. After years of fear, threats and intimidation, how did Communism suddenly fall like a house of cards? That is a great question that has long been debated by some of the brightest minds of our time. Certainly Ronald Reagan, Margaret Thatcher, Pope John Paul II, Lech Walesa, Mikhail Gorbachev and Boris Yeltsin had much to do with it. But the simple answer is that a major transition took place *inside* the hearts of the Communist people, which demanded that they be treated differently from the outside.

Meet the Beatles

When the Beatles made their debut in the mid-1960s, the Russian KGB heard their music and outlawed their albums. The only way to purchase a Beatles album in the USSR in those days was on the black market, where they were sold for more than a hundred dollars each. Why were they outlawed? Because the Russians believed that if their citizens were exposed to the Beatles' music, they would realize there were happy people in the world and overthrow their oppressive government.

It turns out that these fears were not entirely unfounded. In one of the documentaries I watched on the USSR, the commentator actually attributed the end of the Cold War and the fall of Communism to the Beatles.[1] This is a gross exaggeration of the facts, but there is a measure of truth in his point. People are transformed from the inside when they are exposed to new ideas from the outside. Whether these ideas are true or false, internal change takes place as long as the people who are exposed to them embrace the information as accurate. (Of course, transformation in itself is not necessarily positive. The long-term effects of these ideas are primarily determined by whether or not the concepts are actually true.)

It is interesting that we call new ideas *in-formation*. Thoughts really do form structures inside people that eventually demand new structures around them. As internal metamorphosis begins to take place, people's external circumstances, which were once congruent with their lifestyle, become conscious barriers and restrictions to their new sense of purpose and destiny. Ultimately, new mindsets perpetuate transitional epoch season changes, which most often result in forcing governmental shifts. Out of the rubble of such upheavals, new leadership paradigms begin to emerge.

A Lesson from Iraq

Four years after America overthrew Saddam Hussein, I wrote this section about Iraq that you are about to read for the first printing of *Heavy Rain*. At the time, most Americans felt as though the invasion of Iraq had been the right thing to do (although there were some detractors by then). I considered removing it from this revision, until I realized that the concerns I had when I initially wrote this section have actually been playing themselves out right before our eyes. This adds credibility to the points I originally was trying to make throughout this chapter. Because of that, I have decided to include a separate chapter on ISIS, but leave the following paragraphs unedited and untouched, just as I composed them back in 2007.

Great leaders understand that real change can only take place when people are transformed from the inside out, not from the outside in. The invisible kingdom inside a person ultimately becomes the visible kingdom around them. The war in Iraq taught us some profound lessons about this principle. We learned (and are still learning) the hard way that displacing an evil dictator is not nearly as difficult as replacing him. We overthrew Saddam Hussein in 37 days and declared victory on the deck of the aircraft carrier USS *Abraham Lincoln*. But we have spent several more years and the lives of many more soldiers trying to establish a democracy in a region that has been dominated by tyranny for hundreds of years.

The real challenge is how to alter people's worldview when it has been distorted by wrong core values. For example, the highest core value of democracy is freedom that transfers power to the people. The greatest challenge of replacing a dictatorship with a democracy is teaching people who have lived in virtual slavery how to make healthy choices for themselves and by themselves. Free citizens are given the right and the responsibility to make up their own minds, to decide who is going to lead them and to vote for the laws that will guide their society. But often, people who are liberated after being controlled all their lives don't know how to behave in a culture of freedom, and they soon construct other prisons for themselves. The mindset of the Iraqi people has been compounded by the predominant national religion, Islam, which by its very nature creates a culture of control. It requires extreme discipline and submission to leadership. It places little value on freedom, liberty and independence.

On the other hand, like it or not, a democratic government has emerged in Iraq that, at its core, comes from Greek beginnings and is heavily influenced by a Judeo-Christian worldview that values free will over control. (Remember, it is the Christian Bible that teaches us that God put two trees in the Garden. From the beginning of creation, it was the God of the Bible, not the god of the Qur'an, who instituted the concept of free will and choice.) The outcome of Iraq still hangs in the balance, but the greatest battle is not being fought in the streets of Baghdad or any other Iraqi city. The supreme conflict is being waged on the battlefield of the hearts and minds of the country's men and women. The culture that is cultivated inside the souls of its people will ultimately determine the future of Iraq.

A War of Ideas

How is this inner battle fought? What are the weapons of this warfare, and how is victory ascertained? These are the questions great leaders must ask and understand if we are going to be effective in helping create a global reformation. People are transformed as they are exposed to new ideas and embrace them. The need for exposure is obvious; people cannot become what they have not yet seen and/or heard.

The Church understands this very well. We are convinced that preaching the Word of God to people transforms them. But what we often fail to understand is that people only embrace the ideas in which they find value, and they receive ideas best from people who have favor in their lives. The million-dollar question is, how do we get people to value Kingdom ideas when they don't value them already?

Think about it: How did the Beatles propagate their radical new philosophies to the masses? They hid their message in music that everyone loved. People valued the Beatles' melodies, which in turn caused folks to like them. This eventually led the masses to embrace their lyrics. The elements required for true transformation inside people are that they must be exposed to new ideas and they must like the messenger, as well as value the message.

We Christians have a hard time understanding that we only have as much influence in people's lives as they place value on us. Anytime our influence in people's lives transcends the level of value they place on us, they will reject our ideas, and then our ability to bring true change is lost. Actually, people feel manipulated when we try to persuade them beyond the boundaries of the significance we have in their eyes.

A Lesson from Homosexuals

The homosexual community in America has mastered this principle of connecting its agendas with something people value in order to change people's mindsets. Have you ever watched HGTV? It is supposed to be the home improvement channel, but it proclaims a subtle, yet *very powerful* message in its approach to home improvement. The message is that the homosexual lifestyle is normal. Although fewer than 4 percent of Americans are homosexual, a very high percentage of HGTV episodes feature homosexual couples.

Home improvement is a brilliant backdrop for propagating the homosexual agenda. First, it connects straight people who have a similar interest in home improvement with homosexuals. This connection proclaims a hidden message—the idea that heterosexuals and homosexuals have "lots" in common.

Second, it allows the producers to portray homosexual couples in a home setting so that they look like traditional families. Many of the channel's shows portray homosexual couples with their children as they are buying, improving or renovating their homes. The point is clear: "Come in and have a look around. You'll see how much we are like any other married couple. Our family is no different from your family." By attaching this message to something people value, their homes, those advocating homosexuality's "normalcy" gain a platform to expose their audience to their radical ideas.

This strategy is so well thought-out that it astounds me. The majority of HGTV's shows also feature heterosexual people. You might ask, "Why would they show straight couples at all if their agenda is to promote the homosexual lifestyle?" They show both because they know that if HGTV only featured homosexuals on their shows, it would reduce their audience to the small percentage of the population who are already homosexual or are sympathetic to the cause. They would then lose their ability to proclaim their message to the masses.

You can bet that the people at HGTV are not trying to entertain homosexuals; they are trying to convert heterosexuals to their viewpoint. It is gay and lesbian evangelism hidden in the disguise of home improvement. Let me tell you, it is a brilliant plan, and it is working. In the last twenty years, homosexual agendas have leveraged massive control over the climate of our nation. The proponents of these agendas are accomplishing this with just a small pool of the populace. A 2015 Gallup Poll asked Americans what percentage of the population they thought was homosexual. The answers were revealing. The citizens polled thought the percentage of gay and lesbian residents in the United States was somewhere around 23 percent.[2] Remember, it is fewer than 4 percent. (Even the National Gay and Lesbian Task Force estimates that homosexuals are 3 to 8 percent of the population.[3]) It is hard for the average person to conceive that such a small percentage of the population could leverage so much control over a country.

Offending the Masses

Have you ever noticed that unlike the shows on HGTV, most of our religious television programs are produced by Christians, for Christians? Usually, somewhere in the program the producers will throw in some kind of evangelistic message so all the pre-believers who are *not* watching will embrace the Kingdom's cause and get born again.

When are we as Christians going to start being strategic about our influence? We are so darned unstrategic that it is embarrassing. We go to gay pride parades and hold up picket signs protesting their lifestyle in the name of God. I guess we just want to make sure that the homosexual community knows how we feel about their sexual orientation. Boy, those picket signs are having such a huge impact on the gay and lesbian community that they are falling to their knees in the streets and begging God for forgiveness. *Not!*

Sometimes I think we do things as believers just to soothe our consciences. We are not really stupid enough to believe that our protest signs, for instance, are actually influencing gays and lesbians. Picket signs certainly are not what Jesus had in mind when He sent us out to do *signs* and wonders.

To a powerless Church, signs have become something you nail to a stick. I think it just makes us feel as if we are radical Christians when we take a stand for righteousness. It does not seem to occur to us that we are actually hurting our cause by destroying any value we have to the homosexual population. The age-old adage is still true: People don't care what you know until they know that you care.

I was teaching at a ministry school a while back, and as I entered the classroom, some of the students stood in front of the class to share testimonies from an outreach they had done at the downtown mall the day before. The first "testimony" was that the security guards had kicked them out of the mall for trying to minister to customers in the stores. As they recounted the story, the class erupted in shouting, clapping and cheering.

I sat there grieved. There is no glory in offending for no purpose the people we are trying to reach, especially in a country where our right to free speech is protected. The goal is to love people into the Kingdom.

Certainly, you may be rejected in the process of extending that love. Jesus told us not to be surprised by that kind of persecution. He even said, "Blessed are you when men hate you, and ostracize you, and insult you, and scorn your name as evil, for the sake of the Son of Man" (Luke 6:22). But there is a big difference between being hated for the "sake of the Son of Man" and being rejected because we are under the influence of the spirit of stupid, rude or ridiculous.

Some people have a martyr's complex that has perverted their sense of justice. They are under the delusion that anytime they share the Gospel with someone and get the cold shoulder, somehow they got rejected for the cause of Christ. They take the verses about true persecution in the Bible to mean that being disliked by unbelievers is a good sign. But nowhere did Jesus tell us that rejection was the goal. We must not confuse the purpose with the process.

My Story

I have often wanted to find a place to hide while watching certain Christians preach to people. I have been so embarrassed by the way some Christians were treating the very people they were trying to "minister" to. With their attitude, they could have been giving away thousand-dollar bills and they still would have been rejected.

I must be honest, however. My perception of that kind of ministry first developed through my own experience of learning that radical does not mean rude. We need methods that don't undermine our message. In 1977, Kathy and I moved our family from the San Francisco Bay Area to a small community of 3,000 in the mountains of Northern California, where we lived for the next 21 years. We owned several automotive businesses in those days, including a Union 76 service station located on Main Street. In front of the service station, right next to the street, we had a large double-sided reader board where we displayed different quotes or messages every day.

In the late eighties, Planned Parenthood, the leading abortion provider in the country, was determined to put a clinic in our community. The entire Christian community was upset about it. I decided to lead a movement against Planned Parenthood to stop them from establishing a clinic in our town. I thoroughly researched their organization, examining their founder, their history and the impact they had on other cities. Then I put the message PLANNED PARENTHOOD GO HOME on one side of our reader board and ABORTION IS MURDER on the other side. I left that sign up for months.

I went to all the Planned Parenthood community meetings, taking about two hundred Christians with me each time. We completely overpowered the twenty or thirty pro–Planned Parenthood people who attended the meetings. As soon as the Planned Parenthood leaders started to speak, I would stand up, interrupt them and ask them pointed questions. Of course, they could not give an honest or direct answer to any of my questions without being lynched by the pro-life crowd, who cheered and applauded my every question. The Planned Parenthood leaders were quite intimidated by the overall climate of the mob. Who could blame them?

Finally, the issue came to our board of supervisors for a decision. They had to cancel the first meeting and move it to a larger facility to handle the crowds, where again we showed up in overwhelming force. When the supervisors invited the speakers from different perspectives to come to the microphone and share, I spoke for the pro-lifers as they cheered and applauded. When others shared a different point of view, we sneered, booed and let everyone in the room know that we had no respect for them or their opinions. But by the time the meeting was over, the board of supervisors had overwhelmingly voted to allow Planned Parenthood to set up a clinic in our community, where they remain to this day.

I have thought a lot about this experience in an effort to understand it. I still am not sure exactly what happened in the moment of decision that day. I don't know if the people on the board of supervisors were actually voting in favor of Planned Parenthood, or if they were deciding against the disrespect we had been showing our opponents.

Even more sobering to me has been the question of whether or not our attitude tied God's hands and kept Him from acting on our behalf. I am sure we represented His perspectives on the abortion issue accurately, but we sure did not display His heart toward those who disagreed with us. We dishonored, devalued and disrespected those pro-choice people, who were made in God's image, so that we could make our point that they had no value for the human life carried in a woman's womb. To us, the end justified the means. We did not care about the process because we were sure we had the purpose right.

Several years later, I went through a process of identifying and writing down the virtues by which I vowed to live the rest of my life. The fifth virtue on my list came from my experience with Planned Parenthood. It reads: "I will treat all people with respect, whether they are friend or foe, as they were created in God's image." This does not mean that I am opposed to peaceful protesting or other public displays of disapproval. But I am opposed to disrespecting, dishonoring and/or performing acts of hatred toward anyone else, whether I agree with the person's values or not.

Might as Well Join 'Em

On the other end of the spectrum, there is an entire segment of the religious community that is terrified of offending anyone. They have given up on overcoming sin and instead have become just like sinners. They have decided, "If you can't beat 'em, you might as well join 'em."

Of course, they have had to alter the Gospel just a little to embrace things like the homosexual lifestyle and abortion. Not much—only slight changes to the Bible were necessary.

Not! These folks try to stay socially relevant not just by welcoming sinners into their congregations (which all churches should do), but also by *ordaining* them as leaders so that they will not upset anyone. This strategy is just as destructive as violating respect and honor for people when we are proclaiming the Gospel to them. We need to learn how to disagree with someone's sin and still sincerely love and embrace the person.

Jesus did this so well that sinners even invited Him to their drinking parties (see Luke 7:34; 15:1–2). But He never compromised His standards or took on their lifestyle so that they would accept Him. His love for others simply transcended their fear of Him. What a great lesson for all of us.

Denominationalism

I wrote earlier about how denominationalism has affected the way in which Christians relate to one another, causing them to gather when they agree and divide when they disagree. But probably the greatest impact denominationalism has had on our planet is not the way believers treat one another, but the way they relate to the world. Because denominationalism views disagreement as an enemy, the goal of all relational interaction is to convince people, "We are right."

For example, if I have a friendship with a homosexual person, it has to be for the sole purpose of converting that person to "Christianity." The religious community will not give me permission to have a relationship with someone I don't agree with unless I have an agenda. This leads to what I call the "car lot syndrome." When we step onto a car lot and the salesperson approaches us, we all know the drill: "Good afternoon, sir. Lovely day, isn't it? Boy, that's a beautiful pair of jeans you have on. I don't believe I've ever seen a pair of jeans like that before."

And the beat goes on. Everyone knows the salesperson does not give a rip about our jeans, our hair or the fact that we don't sweat much for a heavy person. He or she is just trying to sell us a car.

When we approach non-Christians from our denominational mindset, we carry an agenda. The non-Christians know that we are only in a relationship to sell them Jesus, so nothing we say or do feels sincere to them. But what would happen if we honestly just loved people without an agenda? What would life be like if we had an authentic interest in someone else as a person? This is my new strategy: Love people from the heart and do everything I can to bring out the best in them. It is a pretty radical idea, but I think it just might work.

We must shake off the shackles of denominational mindsets and truly love people regardless of their persuasions. This frees the Lord to commission an army of pure-hearted lovers who can display the raw power of God and demonstrate the superior wisdom of another age—without using manipulation and exploitation. Then He can plant these warriors strategically in the darkest corners of society.

8

Secret Agent Man

We are not called to pound seed into concrete.

Anonymous

We are God's secret agents disguised as doctors, housewives, mechanics, computer programmers, schoolteachers and business managers. We are part of a covert Kingdom. We are powerful believers concealed as everyday people, strategically assigned to serve society while simultaneously destroying the works of the devil. Our very lives are a sign and wonder. Not only do we have the message; we also are the message. To know us is to love us. We are the fruit of God's love, the manifestation of His Person.

To put it in automotive terms, "A great car sells itself." In fact, Jesus described the Kingdom we are part of like this: "The kingdom of heaven is like leaven, which a woman took and hid in three pecks of flour until it was all leavened" (Matthew 13:33).

Could it be that at times we are actually called to be sheep in wolves' clothing? God wants to knead us into society like leaven.

Let me be clear. I am not talking about cowards who call themselves Christians but are afraid to stand up for Christ. Nor am I describing churches that are more sensitive to the will of unbelievers who may attend a Sunday service than they are to the Spirit of God moving among them. There are a lot of counterfeit leavens that masquerade as some Kingdom value.

Jesus put it this way: "Watch out! Beware of the leaven of the Pharisees and the leaven of Herod" (Mark 8:15). At the root of the religious spirit (the leaven of the Pharisees) and the political spirit (the leaven of Herod) is the fear of man. Fear will never lead us to cultural transformation.

Prophetic Mascots

Recently, the hidden nature of this epoch season we are in was reemphasized to me when I taught at our School of Worship. I was gathering my thoughts as I made my way to the podium, and suddenly I heard the Lord say, *Prophesy to the class before you preach to them.*

What's the word You want me to share? I inquired.

The epoch season has changed, and it requires a new prophetic mascot. The prophetic mascot for this hour is no longer the eagle; it's the owl. The owl is nocturnal, so it is designed to live in the night, to see through the darkness and to know who's who. It's the symbol of wisdom, and it feasts on rats, rodents and snakes.

I came to the pulpit and prophesied this word to our students as they listened intently. Just as I finished my declaration, worship leader Jenn Johnson rushed to the front and excitedly took the microphone.

"A student was driving home recently and there was an owl in the middle of the road! It wouldn't move, so he finally got out of his car, picked it up and brought it home with him," Jenn proclaimed, almost jumping out of her skin. "I just called him, and he's bringing the owl to class today."

It is time for the Body of Christ to carry the Kingdom into the darkest places of society. There is a new God-given ability to see through the gloomy, murky and disgusting evil of people's situations to discover the hidden treasures in those who are the Rahabs of life. Like Rahab of old, who worked as a prostitute but became the great-great-great-great-grandmother of Jesus Christ, precious souls who are entangled in the sins of life and covered with the mire of shame and guilt are just waiting to be recovered. It is time for us to join the owl brigade!

The Fall of Babylon

The book of Daniel gives us one of the best examples of cultural transformation birthed out of Kingdom core values. Daniel provides a great pattern for us, demonstrating how God leavens society through His secret agents. The king of Babylon, Nebuchadnezzar, destroyed Israel, tore down the Temple of Solomon and took four young teenagers prisoner to serve at his will. But what Nebuchadnezzar did not realize was that when he arrested Daniel, Shadrach, Meshach and Abednego, God had actually taken Babylon captive.

God initiated His strategic plan for transforming Babylon when Daniel refused to defile himself with the king's wine and choice food and insisted on praying three times a day by kneeling toward Jerusalem (see Daniel 1:8; 6:10). Shadrach, Meshach and Abednego joined the battle when they stared down the spirit of fear by steadfastly refusing to bow down to Nebuchadnezzar's idol in the face of certain death (see Daniel 3:12–18). This insulated them from the prince of the power of the air that was controlling the minds of most of the Babylonian people. It also inoculated them from the cesspool of carnality.

When God saw that He had people who could not be polluted by the evil system around them, He kneaded them into the culture, like leaven into dough, by disguising His four superheroes as magicians and conjurers (see Daniel 1:20). They customized their life to meet the needs of an evil empire without compromising their character. They so assimilated into Babylonian culture that they even took on the names of Babylonian gods. Daniel's name was changed to Belteshazzar, which was the name of Nebuchadnezzar's god (see Daniel 4:8).

Systematically and strategically, these boys began to leverage their Kingdom influence into the hearts of the Babylonians and Persians. Over a period of seventy years, these guys dismantled and displaced the powers of darkness by demonstrating the power and wisdom of a superior Kingdom. Finally, the Persian king, Cyrus, released the people of God to rebuild Jerusalem and restore the Israelites to their land. He even funded the multimillion-dollar Temple project.

Human Rights

King Cyrus the Great was the last in a long line of rulers whom Daniel served. Although Daniel was quite old when he worked for Cyrus, his influence on this king might well be his greatest legacy. Not only is Cyrus the Great credited with the release and restoration of the Israelis, but he is also the father of the concept of human rights. Twenty-five hundred years ago, King Cyrus authored a human rights scroll that has become the prototype for the United Nations.[1] Literally billons of people owe their freedom and equality to a Persian king whose rule Isaiah prophesied years before that king was born (see Isaiah 45:1–7).

Angels guarded this extraordinary king, and Daniel mentored him (see Ezra 1:1; Daniel 10–12). I guess you just really never know who is growing up in your house.

From the opening scene of the story, the superior character, supernatural powers and extraordinary love of Daniel and his three friends continually exposed the Babylonians and the Persian kingdom to another realm. This is the kind of leaven God intends for us to be on the earth—hidden superheroes destroying evil fortresses, influencing kings and making disciples out of every nation. The handwriting is on the wall. God has numbered the devil's kingdom and put an end to it. He has weighed it on the scales and found it deficient. He has handed the world over to the sons of light (see Daniel 5:25–28).

God wants to hide His leaven in every part of society. Not all of us will be assigned to palaces to influence the kings of our day. But whatever sphere of influence God puts us in, we are called to *lead* by putting the superior qualities of the Kingdom on display—the virtues of integrity, honor, compassion, service, power, wisdom and courage. The other dynamic important for us to consider here is that whatever ground we take by force, we will have to maintain through force. But whatever position we gain through honor will be protected by favor.

Discipling Nations

The Body of Christ so desperately needs to learn how to influence society in such a way that people are drawn to us. We have the answers to the world's problems, but we are fumbling our God-given assignment. Our failure to disciple nations is largely a manifestation of our lack of understanding about how to bring true transformation to the lives of people, especially to those who are not hungry for it yet. Jesus commissioned us to *make* disciples of *all* nations and then *teach* them (see

Matthew 28:18–20). The Greek word for disciple, *mathetes*, means "learner." It may surprise some leaders that we are responsible to *create learners* and then *teach them*. I have heard many leaders say things like, "People are just not hungry for the truth." What these leaders don't realize is that although we are not called to "pound seed into concrete," we are responsible to motivate people to want to learn, receive and grow so that we can teach, equip and train them.

Most of us have had an important person in our life who was so passionate about a particular subject that he or she inspired the same interest in us and caused in us a hunger to know more. This is what we are called to do for *all* the nations of the world. Remember, Jesus sent us out as sheep among wolves. The world is hungry for the Body of Christ. They want to consume us. But they need a taste test, a little nibble of the real thing, so that they can become hungry enough to eat His flesh and drink His blood (see John 6:54). When Jesus told people that they must eat His flesh and drink His blood, He was not talking about cannibalism. He was referring to ingesting the Living Word of God. Christ is the Word that became flesh. It is important that we encourage people to ingest Jesus and digest His life, until Christ literally is formed in them. There is an old saying that is true in this case: *You are what you eat.*

Much of the world has ingested the Bible in one form or another, but many have never digested the living, active Word of God. Religion temporarily filled their souls, but it never satisfied their longing for real life. Transformation requires assimilation, not just consumption. The world has had its fill of religion and is fed up with it.

Let me put it this way: For the time being, I am lactose intolerant. When I consume dairy products, my body will not assimilate them into my system. Likewise, many people in the world are Gospel intolerant. When they listen to the preaching of the Word, it has no effect on them—or worse yet, it actually creates a negative reaction in some of them. And then there are others who have consumed just enough religion that it has inoculated them from the real Jesus. Hearing about the Bible without experiencing God leads to having a religious form without any power (see 2 Timothy 3:5). It is like exchanging the Communion meal for a dinner commentary or a cookbook.

We owe the world an encounter with God Himself. When people are exposed to their Creator, they find Him enticing— simply irresistible. We need a strategic plan birthed by the Holy Spirit (a *spirategy*, as I call it) that can bring the Kingdom into every realm of society. We have emphasized the "innocent as doves" part for decades. While holding to this, it is time that we also become as wise as serpents (see Matthew 10:16).

Standing at the Threshold of History

In May 2009, God gave me a profound prophetic word. He said that He had given a certain man a network of churches (He told me the man's name, but I don't want to dishonor him by revealing it here), and that the network had become a catalyst for a worldwide movement. Then the movement became so large and powerful that it began to redefine its fellowship of churches. The leadership of the church network had to decide if they were going to protect their identity or embrace the movement. They chose to protect the fellowship of churches, and they cut off the movement.

In Acts 15, the same scenario was taking place, requiring the same sort of decision. The mother church in Jerusalem was basically Judaism in practice, with Jesus and the Holy Spirit taking center stage. But the Church as a whole was growing and suddenly jumped the firewall of religious tradition, enveloping the Gentiles. The Church then became a catalyst to a movement because, of course, there were many more Gentiles than there were Jews. And to complicate matters even more, the Gentiles who were getting saved were steeped in Greek mythology and polytheism (the worship of many gods). Most of them knew nothing of the Old Testament (the stories of Creation, the Flood and so forth) or of people like Abraham, Isaac, Jacob, Moses, Esther and David. As these Gentiles came into the Kingdom, they began to redefine the Church dramatically.

The apostles called for a leadership summit in Jerusalem to decide what to do. The multitudes listened as the most powerful church leaders in the world wrestled over this dilemma. The discussion began with Paul and Barnabas sharing their incredible stories of God's supernatural intervention in the lives of the Gentiles. Peter followed with his miraculous testimonies of God filling the Gentiles with the Holy Spirit. God was redeeming the Gentiles in the same way that He had saved the Jews, in spite of the fact that they were not keeping all the religious traditions, rules and laws of Judaism.

The apostles had to decide if they were going to let the movement redefine the Church as they knew it, or if they were going to cut off the movement to protect the Jewish identity of the Body. They listened to the Holy Spirit and chose to embrace the movement (see Acts 15:28). James made this historic statement about the Gentile Church: "It is my judgment that we do not trouble those who are turning to God from among the Gentiles, but that we write to them that they abstain from things contaminated by idols and from fornication and from what is strangled and from blood" (Acts 15:19–20). A letter followed that released the Gentiles from having to observe Mosaic Law and Jewish tradition, and the rest is history. From that point on, the Gospel continued to spread more powerfully among the Gentiles, until by AD 100 there were very few Jewish Christians.

Standing at the Same Threshold

The Lord told me that as a Church we are standing at that same threshold in history once again. There is about to be a massive harvest that will be coming from a relatively unreached people group. I believe the Muslims, Hindus and Chinese will comprise a vast portion of this harvest. They will know nothing about the traditions of religion or the foundations of Church history. The Bible itself will be foreign to them, yet the Holy Spirit is going to fall on them in droves. We will be confronted with the same decision that our forefathers faced: Will we cut off the movement to save the Church's identity and reputation, or will we embrace the movement at the risk of being misunderstood by the religious community?

As we cross this historic threshold, it is important to remind ourselves that two thousand years ago our Lord paved the way into this divine paradox. The company He kept seemed to re-define Him to the religious community. They labeled Him a drunkard and a friend of sinners. Religion always seems to find a way to isolate us from the people who need God the most. But we must brave the storms of reputation and reach into the cesspools of darkness, dirtying our hands with the unredeemed souls of men and women.

9

::::::::::::::::::::::::::::::::::

ISIS

Freedom is never more than one generation away from extinction. We didn't pass it to our children in the bloodstream. It must be fought for, protected, and handed on for them to do the same.

Ronald Reagan

There is a threat in the world today that demands our attention. I do mean *demands* our attention! I don't think you can write a book about cultural transformation without addressing the huge elephant in the room, called ISIS or ISIL.[1] And then there is also al-Qaeda. These Muslim radicals are raping our women, beheading our children and torturing and executing our men.

The horror stories seeping out of Iraq and Syria are mind-boggling . . . mothers forced to watch as their children are tortured and killed . . . fathers forced to watch as their daughters are gang-raped and murdered. It is much, much worse than this, but I chose not to disclose all of the details here.

As if this is not bad enough, these Muslim radicals are finding their way into our nations and perpetuating their violent acts on our people. They are leaching their evil ideologies into the fabric of nearly every nation, and they are recruiting our sons and daughters as jihadists.

This worldwide threat has resulted in tens of thousands of deaths, from those at the Twin Towers in New York City to the massacres occurring nearly weekly all around the world today. I was going to name a few of the current ones here, but there are too many. Two more took place while I wrote this chapter.

The "rumors of war" caused by the constant threat assessments, warnings and terrorist dialogue are spreading a relentless sense of impending doom over the globe. It has become commonplace to check the news before you get out of bed in the morning to see where the latest massacre has occurred.

Violence Is Not New

Muslim radicals are not the only violent people we are dealing with in America. School and church shootings, along with other violent outbreaks, are also becoming commonplace in our country.

But for those of us that have been around for a while, violence is nothing new. I was eight years old when President John F. Kennedy was assassinated on November 22, 1963. In the midst of the Vietnam War, Mafia killings and race riots, his brother Senator Robert F. Kennedy was also assassinated, on June 6, 1968. Just two months prior, on April 4, 1968, Martin Luther King was assassinated in Memphis, Tennessee, the day after he gave his famous "I've Been to the Mountaintop" speech.

Those days tested the courage of every American as fear pressed against our souls. We looked on with grief as our leaders were assassinated, race riots filled our streets and our young soldiers' body counts were tallied in the thousands every night on the evening news. All this took place against the backdrop of the threat of a Russian nuclear attack. Consequently, American students practiced their air raid drills every month in school. As I mentioned in chapter 7, I still have vivid memories of the air raid siren blasting its warning in the hallways of my school while I scrambled to get under my desk, my heart beating out of my chest.

About once a week our radios would also blast a warning siren for 60 seconds. At the end of the blast an announcer would repeat, "This is a test of the emergency broadcast system. . . ." If you happened to turn on the radio while the alarm was sounding, you had to wait 60 seconds to find out if it was a test or if we were really under attack. The media played on our fears and did its best to keep us agitated.

Yet things were even worse in my grandparents' day. They lived through two world wars and the Great Depression. World War I went from 1914 to 1918. World War II started September 1, 1939, and ended September 2, 1945. At the same time that the threat of Hitler plagued the world, the Japanese dropped bombs on Pearl Harbor. And as if that were not bad enough, between those two terrible wars America was battered with the Great Depression. For ten long years (1929–1939), our people barely survived. They reached deep into their souls and found the strength to scratch out a living as they persevered through the worst economy in the history of our country.

Of course, if you want to compare the most violent periods in our country's history, you need only go back to 1861, when the Civil War took the lives of 620,000 Americans. I could go on to tell you about the slaughter of the Native Americans, the enslaving of the African Americans or the Revolutionary War, in which we gained our independence from the British at the cost of 50,000 lives.

When you measure the well-being of our country by our past and then you factor in the growth of our population, which has swelled from 31 million in 1861 to 326 million today, America is actually a prosperous place to live at present.

What is my point? I have two. First, when you listen to the media talk, you get the feeling that we are living in the most dangerous time in history. That simply is not true! Do we need to make America (and the world) safer? Yes, of course we do. Our standard is not yesterday's condition; our standard is "on earth as it is in heaven." But as Americans, we live in the most prosperous time in the history of our country.

My second point is that throughout history names change, weapons evolve and conditions fluctuate, yet when hatred, jealousy and bitterness are allowed to seep into people's souls, violence is the inevitable outcome. If we really want to solve the problem, we must therefore deal with people's hearts.

There Is Hope

Twenty-five hundred years ago, a famous prophet named Isaiah saw this deep darkness covering the entire earth. His response to this epic despair was profound and powerful. He wrote,

> Arise, shine; for your light has come, and the glory of the LORD has risen upon you. For behold, darkness will cover the earth and deep darkness the people; but the LORD will rise upon you and His glory will appear upon you. Nations will come to your light, and kings to the brightness of your rising.
>
> Isaiah 60:1

It is not time for us to cower in the corner of adversity; it is time for us to shine! This is our greatest moment. The lights have been dimmed, the stage is set, the characters are prepared, the audience is anxious with anticipation and the curtain is about to open. It is incumbent upon us as the people of God to take a stand. We must turn back this senseless violence and establish beachheads of peace in our world.

"That's great, Kris," you might be asking, "but what does *shine* look like, and what do we do with the violent, crazy people in the meantime?"

These are good questions. It is hard to cure a disease you don't understand, so let's dissect the problem. Let's begin by "looking under the hood" to see if we can begin to comprehend what is driving this intense hatred our enemies feel toward us.

First, it is important to understand who our enemies are and why they are our enemies. There are about 1.7 billion Muslims in the world, so they make up about 23 percent of the earth's population. Most Muslims are peace-loving, normal, everyday people. For the most part, they are embarrassed by the way these wackos are betraying their ethnic origin and their religion. In fact, many Muslims in our country fear the reprisal of other Americans who, with each new act of violence, are growing more intolerant of the peace-loving Muslims' ethnic origin and religion.

It is the *radical* Muslims who view most of the world as their enemy and who typically identify themselves as ISIS, ISIL or al-Qaeda. The good news is that the highest estimates number those who count themselves among the radicals as somewhere in the neighborhood of two hundred thousand people. That means that radical Islamic Muslims only make up about .00012 percent of the entire Muslim population. That does not seem too serious when you consider that the population of the earth is about 7.4 billion people.

Yet the problem actually goes deeper than the relatively small percentage of jihadist Muslims would seem to indicate. Let me explain. According to a poll conducted by a Georgetown Islamic Studies professor and a Gallup pollster, more than one in three Muslims worldwide believe that the 9/11 attacks were "somewhat," "largely" or "completely" justified (23.1 percent say "somewhat," and 13.5 percent say "largely" or "completely"). In other words, even though the number of Muslims who become jihadists is relatively small, a larger percentage of Muslims actually agree with them on some level. This makes the problem quite a bit more complex than it looks on the surface.

The Qur'an

What, exactly, has gone wrong? How do these radical Muslims justify killing innocent people, and why are other Muslims okay with it? Part of the answer lies within the Qur'an, which is the holy book of the Muslim faith. Unlike the Bible, there is no New Testament in the Qur'an, no Savior and no "God so loved the world" passages. Instead, the Qur'an contains at least 109 verses that call Muslims to war with nonbelievers for the sake of Islamic rule. Some of these verses are quite graphic, with commands to chop off people's heads and fingers and kill infidels wherever they may be hiding. Muslims who do not join the fight are called "hypocrites" and are warned that Allah will send them to hell if they do not join the slaughter.

Most of today's Muslims exercise a personal choice to interpret their holy book's call to arms according to their own moral preconceptions about justifiable violence. Apologists cater to their preferences with unsubstantiated arguments that gloss over historical facts and generally do not stand up to scrutiny. Still, it is important to note that the problem is *not* bad people, but bad ideology.

Unfortunately, very few verses in the Qur'an teach tolerance or peace, so there is not much within it to repeal the many verses that call for nonbelievers to be subdued until they accept humiliation, convert to Islam or be killed. In fact, the legacy of Muhammad himself is hostile. Along with the emphasis on violence found in the Qur'an, he and his companions have produced a trail of blood throughout world history.

Here are a few sample verses found in the Qur'an that call Muslims to violence:

O Prophet! strive hard against the unbelievers and the hypocrites and be unyielding to them; and their abode is hell, and evil is the destination.

Qur'an 9:73

And when We wish to destroy a town, We send Our commandment to the people of it who lead easy lives, but they transgress therein; thus the word proves true against it, so We destroy it with utter destruction.

Qur'an 17:16

If the hypocrites, and those in whose hearts is a disease, and the alarmists in the city do not cease, We verily shall urge thee on against them, then they will be your neighbors in it but a little while. Accursed, they will be seized wherever found and slain with a (fierce) slaughter.

Qur'an 33:60–62

Those who disbelieve follow falsehood, while those who believe follow the truth from their Lord. . . . So, when you meet (in fight Jihad in Allah's Cause), those who disbelieve smite at their necks till when you have killed and wounded many of them, then bind a bond firmly (on them, i.e. take them as captives). . . . If it had been Allah's Will, He Himself could certainly have punished them (without you). But (He lets you fight), in order to test you, some with others. But those who are killed in the Way of Allah, He will never let their deeds be lost.

Qur'an 47:3–4

Let me mention one more section of the Qur'an, 18:65–81, which includes a chilling parable. I will not quote the whole parable here, but one interesting website has this to say about it:

> Qur'an 18:65–81 This parable lays the theological groundwork for honor killings, in which a family member is murdered because they brought shame to the family, either through apostasy or perceived moral indiscretion. The story (which is not found in any Jewish or Christian source) tells of Moses encountering a man with "special knowledge" who does things which don't seem to make sense on the surface, but are then justified according to later explanation. One such action is to murder a youth for no apparent reason (74). However, the wise man later explains that it was feared that the boy would "grieve" his parents by "disobedience and ingratitude." He was killed so that Allah could provide them a "better" son. [Note: This is one reason why honor killing is sanctioned by Sharia. Reliance of the Traveler (Umdat al-Saliq) says that punishment for murder is not applicable when a parent or grandparent kills their offspring (o.1.1–2).][2]

Wake-Up Call

What have we learned so far? First, the majority of Muslims—about 70 percent, or 1.2 billion people—hold to a philosophy of peace (for various reasons), even though their holy book actually calls them to violence. Second, very few Muslims get involved in jihad, or holy war, in any manner. It is therefore true from a broad perspective that we are *not* at war with Islam, since the great majority of Muslims are peace-loving people.

Some Americans are angry with President Obama for intentionally playing down (or ignoring) the Muslim component of the terrorist attacks. Personally, I would not want to be at war with 1.7 billion Muslims, and declaring that America is fighting Islam is not only inaccurate; it is stupid! We are *not* at war with Muslims; we are fighting jihadist terrorists. Thankfully, there is a difference.

Furthermore, most of the Muslims in the world are also fighting the terrorists, so in what way are we opposed to Muslims as a people group? I will say it again: All jihadists are Muslims, but most Muslims are not jihadists, nor do they agree with them. And while we are on the subject, the people who are the most affected by the radicals' actions (besides those who are attacked) are probably the peace-loving Muslims. They end up being scrutinized by nearly everyone in society, for obvious reasons.

Yet here is where the water gets muddy, and probably where some people have not used wisdom when they articulate this fine line between the radicals and the rest of the population. Let me use myself as an example. I am of Spanish ethnic origin. If all terrorists were Spanish, even though most Spaniards were *not* terrorists I would expect to come under greater scrutiny than most of the population.

In the case of the Muslims, you have to add to the equation that being Muslim is not genetic, as is being Spanish, but rather it is a belief system (a religion) people choose to embrace. That in itself intensifies the need for scrutiny. And finally, you have to realize that the Islamic religion is based on a book that encourages violence toward nonbelievers. Given that fact, I am not sure how those working for anti-terrorist agencies could justify not focusing most of their efforts on people who identify themselves as Muslims.

Let me make one more point before we talk about some solutions. Jihadists are provoked by the fact that there are "infidels" in the world whom they believe must be converted or killed. Contrary to popular opinion, the root of the jihadists' violence lies in their belief system; they are not reacting to those whom they deem infidels.

In other words, the idea that America, Europe, Russia or anyone else is provoking the radical Muslims to violence is a myth. It simply is not true. Radical jihadists like those who make up ISIS are motivated to destroy both non-Muslims and Muslims who refuse to be jihadist, because the Qur'an teaches these radicals to hate "infidels." No one is provoking them; they are not reacting to anyone. Unquestionably, they are responding to their holy book. That is it . . . period . . . end of story![3]

What Is the Solution?

What is the solution to all this? The only way to stop the jihadists' hatred is for them to change their ideology—their core belief system. Jesus warned us about people like them when He said, "But an hour is coming for everyone who kills you to think that he is offering service to God" (John 16:2). The immediate application of this verse involved the radical Jews who crucified Christ, and later the Romans who killed Christians in the Coliseum. But the jihadists fit perfectly into this category, in that they kill people to please Allah (their god).

Saul of Tarsus was the equivalent of a first-century ISIS leader, although he was a radical Pharisee, not a Muslim jihadist. He was leading a sect of Pharisees who were dragging Christian men, women and children into the city squares and stoning them to death. It is not clear how many deaths he personally was responsible for, but likely it numbered in the thousands.

Saul's deadly escapade ended abruptly when he had a supernatural encounter with Jesus on the road to Damascus. He not only ceased persecuting believers; as the apostle Paul, he also became one of the greatest Christian leaders in history (see Acts 9:1–22). As he later wrote in one of his epistles, where sin abounds, grace abounds all the more (see Romans 5:20).

Prayer Strategy

The roots of our struggle against this evil lie in a realm that most people cannot see, but that we all experience. The apostle Paul gave us some great insight into this battle in the book of Ephesus, where he wrote, "Our struggle is not against flesh and blood, but against the *rulers*, against the powers, against the world forces of this darkness, against the spiritual forces of wickedness in the heavenly places" (Ephesians 6:12, emphasis added).

I would like to point out that Paul was not warring with demons; he was struggling against principalities. Principalities are high-level beings in the demonic realm who affect global conditions. That means world changers are struggling with world forces of darkness. I also want to call your attention to the word *rulers* in this passage because I think understanding it will open up a world of revelation to us and help us defeat this evil enemy. The word *rulers* is the Greek word *arche*, which means beginnings, origins, elementary teachings, first preaching, principalities and rulers. Interestingly enough, Paul uses the same word in his letter to the Philippians: "You yourselves also know, Philippians, that at the *first preaching* of the gospel . . ." (Philippians 4:15, emphasis added). The two words *first preaching* in this passage are actually translated from the Greek word *arche*.

In the same way that Paul taught the Philippians about the origins (the foundations, the beginnings) of life, there is a principality named *arche* that is in charge of redefining the foundations of all truth. We see this spirit at work in many different arenas throughout the world. For example, *arche* is redefining the origins of life so that many people no longer think we are created in the image of God; instead, they think we are an evolved form of apes.

Another important origin in question involves the human fetus. There is much debate over whether or not a fetus is a human being. *Arche* has convinced the world that a human fetus is just tissue, which can easily be disposed of without consequences. If a woman gives birth to it, then it is a baby, but if she aborts it, then it is fetal tissue.

Do you know anything else that is defined by its outcome instead of by its conception? It sounds crazy, but that is the power of *arche*. This spirit is even teaching people a new way to define the origin of what constitutes gender. Even though a person may have a penis and biologically be a male, if "he" feels like a female, then "he" is one.

Again, *arche* has tremendous power to take an irrational concept and convince normal, everyday people that it makes perfect sense. *Arche* is one of the spirits at work in the jihadists that causes them to think that torturing, raping and murdering people is somehow pleasing to God.

With all this in mind, I have developed a prayer strategy regarding the radical Muslims. It is a multipronged approach:

1. Adopt a terrorist. Find out the name of a terrorist from the FBI's Most Wanted list and begin to pray that the person will have God encounters. Ask the Holy Spirit to give you specific things to pray and prophesy over the person while you are in your prayer closet.

2. Pray for the truth of God to be released through the Holy Spirit, and that the angels reinforce this truth to Muslims. But especially, pray for the Allamah (the scholars of the Islamic religion) to know the truth that sets them free.

3. Pray for terrorists everywhere to have supernatural encounters, but especially pray for their leaders. One Damascus road encounter happening to the right leader literally could shift the entire atmosphere away from terrorism.

4. Pray that every terrorist attack be thwarted. Pray for the terrorist to be apprehended, for guns to misfire and for bombs to fail. Ask the Lord to confuse the plans of the terrorists, and to bewilder, perplex and distract them in the midst of their evil deeds.

5. A house divided against itself cannot stand. Pray that the Lord would cause the terrorists to turn against one another so that they would not get along and would refuse to trust one another.

6. Pray for our leaders to have wisdom and for our prophets to have insight into the schemes of the terrorists. Ask God to provide supernatural insights to the Department of Homeland Security, the FBI and the Secret Service, along with all of our local authorities.

Obviously, this is not an exhaustive list of terrorist prayer targets, nor is it the last word on strategic insights into the cure for Islamic jihad. Nevertheless, it might be the beginning of a catalytic journey into unleashing heaven on the dark world of destructive religion. Fervent prayer shapes the course of history.

Is Violence Necessary?

I hate violence. I think it is an ineffective way to resolve problems, and it does not actually cure the root issues of society's brokenness. Violence is terrible . . . there are just no two ways about it.

That being said, I think there is a lot of confusion about whether or not we should protect people by using force. Oftentimes, people quote Jesus' exhortation to turn the other cheek as validation that we should not meet violence with violence (see Matthew 5:39). Or they quote His exhortation to love your enemies as a reason that force is never an acceptable way to deal with certain vicious people (verse 44).

I think there is also a huge misunderstanding, however, about the difference between the role of government and our personal attitude toward our enemies. Let's look at that more closely by examining the most commonly quoted nonviolence passage in the Bible. Then we will contrast it with some other passages. In fact, Jesus contrasts the Old Testament's "eye for an eye" attitude toward people with the New Testament's command to love everyone.

Let's read the nonviolence passage so that we feel the weight of our responsibility to display the love of God no matter how people treat us. Jesus starts by quoting the Law of Moses: "You have heard that it was said, 'An eye for an eye, and a tooth for a tooth.' But I say to you, do not resist an evil person; but whoever slaps you on your right cheek, turn the other to him also" (Matthew 5:38–39).

This "turn the other cheek" attitude is a great revelation of the power of the Cross. This is one of the important core beliefs that separates radical Christians from radical Muslims. Let's remember a few things about Jesus and His Kingdom: The high standard of the love of Jesus transcends the deepest hate any enemy can muster. We must *never* allow hate to seep into our souls. And hate can never be a factor in the way we deal with anyone, including our enemies.

Now let's contrast the way in which Jesus, as a world leader, deals with evil nations that abuse their people: "From His [Jesus'] mouth comes a sharp sword, so that with it He may strike down the nations, and He will rule them with a rod of iron; and He treads the wine press of the fierce wrath of God, the Almighty" (Revelation 19:15).

I think it is clear that Jesus relates to people differently than He relates to nations. This would be especially true of evil kingdoms that are bent on destruction. Contrary to popular opinion, Jesus is not a Buddhist. He is not a pacifist or an anti-war peacekeeper, humming to Himself in a garden somewhere. In fact, Jesus is not a peacekeeper at all; He is a *peacemaker*, and there is a huge difference. *Peacekeepers* spend their time trying to keep everybody happy, while *peacemakers* bring forth truth that destroys lies, exposes false religions and releases hope into its hearers' hearts. Paul said it best; "The God of peace will soon crush Satan under your feet" (Romans 16:20).

Sometimes it takes an act of violence to bring peace to a situation. Those who think Jesus is passive need only remember that He is the one who said, "My kingdom is not of this world. If My kingdom were of this world, then My servants would be fighting so that I would not be handed over to the Jews; but as it is, My kingdom is not of this realm" (John 18:36).

Love Has Many Faces

Jesus is both the Lion and the Lamb, because love has many faces. It looks like different things in different situations. Let's look at another situation that is a little less volatile than the ISIS issue. I had a family member who refused to work and instead asked us for money all the time. What would Jesus do? That is a great question. Does the answer lie in the passage that follows the "turn the other cheek" verse? Jesus went on to say, "Give to him who asks of you, and do not turn away from him who wants to borrow from you" (Matthew 5:42).

It looks as if there is only one answer. If I have the where-withal to help, then I am to provide my family member with all the money he needs to live. Problem solved.

Not so fast! The apostle Paul wrote in his instructions to Timothy, "If anyone does not provide for his own, and especially for those of his household, he has denied the faith and is worse than an unbeliever" (1 Timothy 5:8). Paul also wrote, "If anyone is not willing to work, then he is not to eat, either. For we hear that some among you are leading an undisciplined life, doing no work at all, but acting like busybodies" (2 Thessalonians 3:10–11). Add to that Solomon's words: "Appetite is an incentive to work; hunger makes you work all the harder" (Proverbs 16:26 MESSAGE).

Burt if I don't give my family member money because he refuses to work, am I disobeying Jesus? No. In fact, sometimes giving people a handout undermines their progress.

My point is that there are times when love requires us to turn the other cheek, and there are other times when love must get tough and stop enabling evil.

The Purpose of Government

The prophet Isaiah had some profound things to say about the responsibility and authority of government. He wrote, "There will be no end to the increase of His government or of peace. . . . The zeal of the LORD of hosts will accomplish this" (Isaiah 9:7). The two things we learn here from Isaiah are that the government of God is ever increasing and that the purpose or fruit of God's government is peace.

Government is commissioned with the authority and tasked with the responsibility of bringing peace and keeping peace among the nations. But practically speaking, how does government do this? Paul's words to the Romans are extremely insightful:

> Every person is to be in subjection to the governing authorities. For there is no authority except from God, and those which exist are established by God. Therefore whoever resists authority has

138

opposed the ordinance of God; and they who have opposed will receive condemnation upon themselves. For rulers are not a cause of fear for good behavior, but for evil. Do you want to have no fear of authority? Do what is good and you will have praise from the same; for it is a minister of God to you for good. But if you do what is evil, be afraid; for it does not bear the sword for nothing; for it is a minister of God, an avenger who brings wrath on the one who practices evil. Therefore it is necessary to be in subjection, not only because of wrath, but also for conscience' sake. For because of this you also pay taxes, for rulers are servants of God, devoting themselves to this very thing. Render to all what is due them: tax to whom tax is due; custom to whom custom; fear to whom fear; honor to whom honor.

Romans 13:1–7

Paul makes seven important points about government in this passage:

1. Government derives its authority from God Himself because He establishes it. Leaders therefore have responsibility and authority over other people.
2. Whoever resists governmental authority is resisting God Himself.
3. Government is a "minister of God," and those who are employed to carry out their governmental obligations are "servants" of God.
4. People who are evil or who do evil should be afraid of those in authority because government is an avenger, commissioned to bring wrath upon evildoers.
5. Government bears the sword for the purpose of using it against evildoers.
6. God authorized governments, established for the purpose of keeping order and bringing peace to society, to fund themselves through taxes paid by the people.
7. We are to honor governmental leaders for their position.

An incident that took place in our country recently perfectly exemplifies the point I am making. An assassin went into a shopping mall with an AK-47 and hundreds of rounds of ammunition. He began randomly shooting people as they fled for their lives in panic. Peace finally came when the police shot the man dead. Was it wrong for the police to kill a man to save the lives of many others? No, absolutely not! Were the police giving him an "eye for an eye"? No. Their motive was not to judge the man, but to protect the people. Love always protects the innocent.

Passivity Is Not the Kingdom

Now let me bring my point home. If a serial killer is loose in your city, everybody in the community is probably on edge. They all want the serial killer stopped before more people are hurt. But what if he happens to break into your house? Would you call 911 while you are praying? If the killer made his way into your children's bedroom before the police arrived, would you defend your children, no matter the cost? If the police arrived and could not stop him with words, would you want them to use force?

I bet your answer to all these questions is yes. The truth is that Jesus wants you to protect your family and defend your children. In His discourse about staying alert because He is coming like a thief in the night, He used an example that everyone can relate to. He said, "But be sure of this, that if the head of the house had known at what hour the thief was coming, he would not have allowed his house to be broken into" (Luke 12:39). Jesus' point was to stay alert, yet His choice of examples still validates the fact that you don't just pray for thieves; you prepare yourself to resist them. Personally, I want perpetrators arrested before they get into my house, not after they get in. In other words, I want law enforcement to proactively find them and stop them.

Rwanda, Africa, is a perfect example of what happens when government refuses to carry out its God-given mission. I visited Rwanda for the first time in 2004. A violent genocide had taken place there ten years earlier. Nearly one million people had been slaughtered with machetes—women, babies, children, men—everybody literally had been hacked to death in the streets. Why hadn't anyone stopped this senseless killing? Actually, the United Nations peacekeeping troops had fled the country because they did not want to get involved.

It would have been important to pray for God to uproot the hatred in people's hearts during those terrible days, and people did pray. In fact, 95 percent of the Rwandan people are churchgoing Christians. They needed the government to act and take on its responsibility of protecting the people, until the hearts of the perpetrators had time to be transformed. But that did not happen. Instead, blood ran down the gutters of their streets for one hundred days and nights. God, forgive us!

In a less intense example that is closer to home, years ago I ran a youth group for juvenile delinquents who were on parole with the Trinity County Probation Department. I met with those kids twice a week for five years. The very first night, I broke up five fistfights. Those kids refused to respond to a few Bible verses and flowers. I had to use force to break up the fights; nothing else worked. Talking to them while they were trying to kill each other was meaningless.

That scene repeated itself over and over for the first couple of years. As time went on, I taught the kids life skills such as how to resolve conflict peacefully. I don't remember a single fight during the last three years I was there. The kids had learned that violence was not the answer. But in the beginning, I often tackled them to the floor and held them down until they agreed to leave. Trust me, it was not pretty. In fact, it was scary. Oftentimes, my Christian friends would come down to "help." But usually, after one night of violent encounters they were done. It was hard for these helpers to grasp that passivity is not the Kingdom.

America's Sheltered Lives

I honestly think that many people in my country grow up in a sheltered environment and therefore live with rose-colored glasses on. They seem to have no idea what the real world is actually like. The closest they have ever gotten to violence is seeing an R-rated movie.

These are often the same people who are protesting American "violence" against ISIS. The irony of this is that our police are often in the streets to protect these protestors. And if the protestors feel as though the cops have mistreated them, they are the first to go nuts, demanding their rights and screaming about police brutality.

The funny thing is, they are protesting the idea of the American government trying to protect innocent people from being murdered by the thousands in cold blood, yet at the same time they want justice for their supposed mistreatment by the very government that they are protesting. Now, that is stupid! If these American citizens want our government to turn the other cheek abroad, then at the least they need to demonstrate the same attribute themselves at home.

I am thankful that these passive people were not around when Adolf Hitler was torturing Jews in front of their own families and murdering them by the millions in gas chambers. I am sorry, but terrorists must be stopped. We have to develop a prayer strategy that ultimately transforms Muslims, especially the radicals. But in the meantime, love demands that we protect the innocent. In fact, Jesus said, "Greater love has no one than this, that one lay down his life for his friends" (John 15:13). Jesus laid down His life through a violent act of grace. He died in an act of violence to deliver us from sin, defeat our enemy and give us abundant life.

Sometimes we are called to "Suffer hardship . . . as a good soldier of Christ Jesus" (2 Timothy 2:3). We cannot wait until the terrorists come to our towns to defeat them. We must assist other countries proactively in defeating them. Otherwise, five years from now your children will be fighting them in our streets. We have to make the cost of joining terrorist cells so high and the reward so minuscule that it makes no sense whatsoever to join them. This is what governments are commissioned to do in these times—bring the wrath of God on those who choose evil, so that others will fear doing the same. (I am simply repeating Paul's words to the Romans.)

My country is blessed, but it is not perfect. Our history is riddled with numerous mistakes, many of which we covered up with lies. But we cannot wallow in our past regrets, nor can we become lethargic about our future destiny. It is incumbent upon us as the people of God to embrace both the Lamb and the Lion, so that we respond with wisdom and vigilance to the dangers that lie before us.

We can defeat this terrorist enemy we face in our time from the inside out. But until then, we must stop the senseless murder of innocent people. We must rescue the powerless and defeat the wicked. As Jesus said in Luke 12:48, "From everyone who has been given much, much will be required."

10

:::

The Tipping Point

You will never possess what you are unwilling to pursue.

Mike Murdock

In his bestselling book *The Tipping Point*, Malcolm Gladwell recounts the now classic story of mindless crowd-think revealed in the report of a young woman named Kitty Genovese, who was brutally raped and murdered in 1964 in Queens, New York. The most shocking part of the story was that, according to the *New York Times* report, 38 of her neighbors witnessed Genovese desperately fighting for her life. Though the incident lasted more than half an hour, not one of them intervened or *even called the police.*

This report provoked various investigations into what two scientists have termed the "bystander problem." Their studies revealed that if one person witnesses a crime, it is likely that he or she will get involved. But as the number of witnesses grows, the chances of intervention drastically decrease. The apparent reason for this, Gladwell writes, is that "when people are in a group . . . responsibility for acting is diffused."[1]

This bystander problem is also called the crowd syndrome. Everyone thinks that everyone else has made the call, and consequently, no one does anything. Former president Ronald Reagan famously said, "To sit back hoping that someday, some way, someone will make things right is to go on feeding the crocodile, hoping he will eat you last—but eat you he will." When we choose not to make that 911 call, we had better remind ourselves that we might become the next victim.

Stray Sheep and Monkey Business

The Bible addresses this social dynamic when it says, "All of us like sheep have gone astray" (Isaiah 53:6; see also 1 Peter 2:25). How do sheep go astray? They spend all their time watching each other's butts, hoping that there is a shepherd in front of the flock somewhere. We all suffer from this ultimate crowd deception at times. We get so used to the scenery that we develop a strange security in rump watching. Just the motion itself is mesmerizing. It is a career opportunity for some; for others, it is a hobby, like birdwatching. You can always recognize the rump watchers, because they are saying things like, "Well gosh, Mildred, we must be going the right way. Look at all those butts ahead of us. I mean, golly, all those butts can't be wrong, can they?"

I know the prophet Chiquita said, "The banana that leaves the bunch is the one that gets eaten." But for crying out loud, can we learn to think a little, please? When people stop thinking for themselves, they cut off the flow of invention, innovation and advancement. This creates a stale culture where traditions and rituals lose their significance, mostly because no one can remember why on earth they are doing them.

This reminds me of the "five monkey" experiment I heard about a couple of years ago. The experiment starts with a cage containing five monkeys. Inside the cage a banana on a string is hanging over a set of stairs. Before long, a monkey goes to the stairs and starts climbing toward the banana. As soon as he touches the stairs, all the other monkeys are sprayed with cold water. After a while, another monkey makes an attempt with the same result—the other monkeys are sprayed with cold water. Pretty soon when another monkey tries to get the banana, the other monkeys try to prevent that monkey from doing so.

Eventually, the cold water is removed along with one of the monkeys, which is replaced with a new monkey. The new monkey sees the banana and goes to climb the stairs. To the new monkey's horror, the other monkeys attack it. After another futile attempt, it realizes that if it touches the stairs, it will be assaulted.

Next, another of the original five monkeys is removed and replaced with a new one. The newcomer heads toward the stairs and finds itself under attack. The previous newcomer joins in the punishment with enthusiasm. Then a third monkey is replaced with a new one, and then a fourth and then the fifth. Every time a newcomer takes to the stairs, it is attacked.

By this point, most of the monkeys beating up the new monkey have no idea why they were not permitted to climb the stairs when they tried or why they are participating in the beating. After replacing all the original monkeys, none of the remaining monkeys has ever been sprayed with cold water. Still, no monkey ever again approaches the stairs.

"Why not?" you may ask. Because as far as they know, "That's the way it's always been done around here!"

It is time to question reality. It is important to ask ourselves why we do the things we do. Is it possible that the conditions that caused us to keep certain important traditions have changed?

Has deeper revelation or new technology made the customs in which we take so much pride and from which we get so much comfort irrelevant? It is time that we transition from a stereotype to a prototype.

I Have Decided

I have decided to think for myself. I am not rebellious or independent, nor do I want to reinvent the wheel, so to speak. But I will not let Rush Limbaugh, Sean Hannity, Piers Morgan, Ed Schultz, Bill O'Reilly or anyone else, for that matter, think for me.

It is not that I don't appreciate other people's opinions. I really do learn a lot from others. It is just that I am no one's puppet. I have been commanded to arise and *shine*, not arise and *reflect* (see Isaiah 60:1).

I have been called to be a voice, not an echo. I refuse to be reduced to a political affiliation, a denomination, a generation, a geographic location, my sexual orientation or my ordination. I will not settle for becoming a cheap imitation of another instead of an original of myself. I will not be condensed to a history lesson, nor will I allow someone's fear to constrain my own exploits. I will not bow down to anyone's idol or be conformed to old religious ideologies that will render me irrelevant to the Kingdom.

On the other hand, it is not my desire to become a maverick or a heretic who exchanges the solid foundation of time-tested truth for the test tube of isolation. I therefore will allow the Holy Spirit to lead me, guide me and correct me. I will submit to true leadership and remain moldable, teachable and humble. I will love passionately, live zealously, work wholeheartedly, laugh joyfully and be completely spent at the end of my life. I will walk powerfully, pray unceasingly, give extravagantly and serve God with my whole being.

Expert Advice

It takes courage to break ranks with religious clones and think for ourselves. But we must realize that creativity, imagination and real learning are never cultivated in crowds. We also have to recognize that there are no permanent "arrivals" or plateaus in this life. Either we are growing, expanding and developing, or we are declining, stagnating and petrifying. No matter how much you have seen, experienced and learned, there is always more, always a new frontier that requires courage to explore. If you stop living on this edge of continuous growth and expansion, you risk cutting yourself off from your potential in God.

Bill Johnson says, "What you know can keep you from what you need to know." He is right, because as soon as you consider yourself an expert, you stop learning and growing. The Pharisees are a great example of people who memorized the Word of God, yet did not recognize the Author of the Book when He stood right in front of them explaining it to them. History is full of experts whose imagination was imprisoned by their education, experience or fear of rejection. Consider some of the following examples:

- "Man will never reach the moon regardless of all future scientific advances." (Dr. Lee DeForest, father of radio and grandfather of television)
- "The bomb will never go off. I speak as an expert in explosives." (Admiral William Leahy, U.S. Atomic Bomb Project)
- "The wireless music box has no imaginable commercial value. Who would pay for a message sent to nobody in particular?" (David Sarnoff Associates, response to urgings for investment in radio, 1920s)
- "Heavier-than-air flying machines are impossible." (Lord Kelvin, president of the Royal Society, 1895)

- "I think there is a world market for maybe five computers." (Thomas Watson, chairman of IBM, 1943)
- "Drill for oil? You mean drill into the ground to try and find oil? You're crazy!" (Drillers that Edwin L. Drake tried to enlist to his project to drill for oil, 1859)
- "We don't like their sound, and guitar music is on the way out." (Decca Recording Co. rejecting the Beatles, 1962)
- "I'm just glad it'll be Clark Gable who falls on his face, not Gary Cooper." (Gary Cooper, on his decision not to take the leading role in *Gone with the Wind*)
- "I don't know what use anyone could find for a machine that would make copies of documents. It certainly couldn't be a feasible business by itself." (Head of IBM, refusing to back the idea, forcing the inventor to found Xerox)
- "Louis Pasteur's theory of germs is ridiculous fiction." (Pierre Pachet, Professor of Physiology at Toulouse, France, 1872).[2]

Add to that list the 1923 Nobel Prize winner who said that man would never tap the power of the atom; the 1949 *Popular Mechanics* article that said that with advancements yet to come, computers might end up weighing no more than 1.5 tons; the publishing house editor who said in 1957 that data processing was no more than a fad; the IBM engineer who asked with all sincerity in 1968 what on earth a microchip would be good for; the 1876 Western Union memo that determined the "telephone" device had too many shortcomings to have any value; the British surgeon who said in 1873 that the human abdomen, chest and brain would be forever shut off from medical intrusion by surgeons; the founder of a large corporation who said in 1977 that there was no reason anyone would want a computer in their home; the critic who said that founding a cookie store like Mrs. Fields' Cookies in America was a bad idea because as a country we like crispy cookies, not chewy ones; and the U.S. patent commissioner who said in 1899 that everything that could be invented had been invented.

Looking at these examples, where do you think we would be today if people always let the "experts" dictate the boundaries of their imagination? How different would society be if the history makers had followed the crowd or had allowed their ideas to be judged in the courtroom of popular opinion? It takes a deep thinker to realize there are eggs that were meant to fly!

The Four-Minute Mile

On May 6, 1954, Roger Bannister broke the four-minute mile. Until he did, the four-minute mile was considered not merely unreachable, but, according to the physiologists of the time, dangerous to the health of any athlete who attempted to reach it. Scientists told runners that it was physically impossible to run a mile in under four minutes. As a result, for thousands of years no athletes ever ran a mile in under four minutes.

When Bannister crossed the finish line in 3 minutes, 59.4 seconds, he broke through the veil of the impossible. Six weeks later, on June 21, 1954, John Landy broke Bannister's record. By 1957, sixteen other runners had broken the four-minute mile.

What happened to the *physical* barrier that prevented humans from running a mile in under four minutes? Was there a sudden leap in human evolution? No. It was the *change in thinking* that made the difference. Bannister proved that it was possible to break the four-minute mile.

Often, the difference between what is and what could be is not measured by the length of the track, but rather by the resistance between our ears. The impossible barriers we perceive are frequently just obstacles in our own minds. Previous runners had been held back by their belief system and mindset. When

Bannister and then Landy finally broke the spell, sixteen other runners saw that it was possible and went on to do the same thing. Since then, hundreds of athletes have broken the four-minute mile. One man had a showdown with fear and gunned it down on the streets of mediocrity. More than five decades later, people are still feeling the effects of his courage.

One City

It astounds me that one person's breakthrough can have such a powerful ripple effect in the sea of humanity. Bill Johnson had an experience several years ago that proved to me that Roger Bannister was more than a great athlete; he was a prophetic symbol of the way God wants to transform cities. Bill went to an all-day prayer meeting in Vacaville, California, which is about two hours from Redding. The event was already in session when Bill arrived, so he settled into a place to pray with the other intercessors as they stormed heaven for earth's reformation. After some time, a well-known prophet approached Bill with a prophetic word.

"Bill," he said, "I believe that God is looking for one city that would be completely His. God wants to cause a breakthrough in one city that affects every realm of society. When that one city falls under the power of God, it will create a domino effect across the entire world that will result in city after city being brought into the Kingdom."

"I believe that city is Redding, California!" Bill responded.

A few minutes later, another seasoned prophetess came to Bill and whispered in his ear, "Bill, I think that God is looking for one city that would be completely His. If God finds one city that welcomes His presence in every place in society, it will cause a domino effect and hundreds of cities all around the world will come into the Kingdom."

Bill started to say, "I believe——" but before he could finish, she interrupted, "I believe that city is Redding!"

Could Redding—or your city—be the tipping point of historic exploits? Is it possible that one city could break through the barrier of naysayers and doubters, as Roger Bannister did with running the four-minute mile? Will history record a massive global revival that dramatically lowers the crime rate to the point where children can play in the streets at night again? Could such an event reduce the divorce statistic, cause us to speak of cancer in the past tense, like smallpox, and so stimulate the economy through generosity that there literally would be no poor among us?

Could the transformation go so deep and be so broad that joy would fill every home? Could its effects mean that people would stop abusing their children, and we would all consider abortion a barbaric, inhumane act, like cannibalism? Could it mean that immoral businesses like drugs and pornography would dry up?

What if signs and wonders became so frequent that God's glory literally hovered over cities like a mist, and "sinners" became a very small minority group? We believe that Redding is destined to fulfill all these dreams, and we are praying, working and living to that end. To borrow a line from John Lennon, "You may say I'm a dreamer, but I'm not the only one."[3] Maybe someday you will join us, and the world will live *and be won* (my play on words).

Democracies Rule?

Democratic culture perpetuates the illusion that it is not the Roger Bannisters of the world who create breakthroughs, but the crowd that is most often right. The masses rule, and the will of the majority determines history. But as Malcolm Gladwell so profoundly pointed out with his true illustration of a crime where none of the witnesses came forward to help, crowds rarely act. Mobs become swamps—stale, murky waters of inaction.

Believers who grow up in democratic countries often live under the delusion that the Kingdom is a democracy. We forget that God refers to Himself as King, not President. For example, we think that if we can rally a million people to pray in Washington, D.C., then certainly God will have to move on behalf of our nation. Personally, I love to see Christians get together for anything and I support large gatherings, but the Kingdom of God is not a democracy; it is a theocracy.

When Judah was in trouble, God commanded the prophet Jeremiah, "Roam to and fro through the streets of Jerusalem, and look now and take note. And seek in her open squares, if you can find *a man*, if there *is one* who does justice, who seeks truth, then I will pardon her" (Jeremiah 5:1, emphasis added). The majority does not rule in the natural world, as we saw in chapter 7 with my example of the gay community being highlighted on HGTV, and God is not moved by the masses in the unseen realm, either. The Lord does not look down from heaven and take a head count to see who is on the side of a particular issue so that He can act. Believe it or not, He is not the cosmic pollster. Can you imagine Jesus saying to Gabriel, "Well, Gabe, it looks as if we finally got a majority of believers to agree with us on that marriage issue; you can go ahead and intervene on that thing now"? That is ridiculous, yet it is the predominant mindset of the Church.

God continues to say, as He has always said, "Find Me a man, a woman, a son or a daughter. Just find Me someone who is fed up, fired up and filled up." God told the Israelites, "The eyes of the LORD move to and fro throughout the earth that He may strongly support those whose heart is completely His" (2 Chronicles 16:9).

God is not looking for a crowd; He is longing for a person. He is not wowed by the masses or mesmerized by the multitudes. Neither is He put off by the powerless. He just needs someone to step out of the crowd and make that phone call. He is simply longing once again for a person like David to emerge from the wilderness and let the giants of life know that they have *messed with the wrong guy. They have taunted the armies of the living God.* When we step out of the crowd and become God's courageous people, we create tipping points where breakthrough is inevitable.

11

Unreasonable Courage

The difference between those who do something and those who don't is that those who do something . . . do something!

Banning Liebscher

It is important for us to realize that along with apostolic mantles and strategic missions, it will also take unreasonable courage to break out of the secure prison of powerless religion and the mindless thinking of the crowd, and move into the prevailing place of global influence. Despite popular opinion, movements never define people. Men and women define movements. In 1955, a 42-year-old Southern black woman, exhausted from a hard day at work, refused to sit in the back of a transit bus. The bus driver warned her that her defiance would give him cause to call the police and have her arrested. But she had had enough of white bigotry. She knew that as long as she submitted to it, she was allowing injustice to continue. She bravely did the right thing and faced the consequences. Her name was Rosa Parks.

Rosa stepped out of the crowd and made the call. She was not a part of a movement. There was no movement. Instead, she put her shoulder into the boulder of history and gave it a shove. And history not only moved—it is still moving. Later in life Rosa wrote, "Without a vision the people perish, but without courage dreams die."

When a young preacher named Dr. Martin Luther King Jr. got involved in the civil rights movement, he wanted to create a peaceful revolution. People told him he was crazy. They said there was no such thing as social change without acts of violence. Dr. King refused to listen to them. A while later, some radical white supremacists bombed his house. He was home with his wife and young daughter when the explosion went off. The blast ripped through their house, tearing off its entire front and narrowly missing his family. Within minutes, angry black militants arrived and tried to convince Dr. King to fight back with violence. But he stood on the rubble of what was once his front porch and proclaimed forgiveness for the perpetrators. The rest is history: a man, a dream and his God.

Then there was Winston Churchill. We need to be like him in our approach. He famously said, "History will be kind to me, for I intend to write it."

Inventory Your Strengths

One of the main reasons people don't act is because they feel an overwhelming sense of inadequacy. It is so easy to inventory our weaknesses and disqualify ourselves from the historic exploits God has assigned to each of us. We forget that Jesus borrowed a couple of fish and some bread from a boy's lunch box and fed a multitude (see John 6:1–14). The crowd did not eat rice and beans, because the boy had brought fish and loaves. Jesus multiplied what the boy had, not what he did not have. God does not care about what you don't have. He only cares about what you *do* have. Theodore Roosevelt put it like this:

> It is not the critic who counts; not the man who points out how the strong man stumbled or where the doer of deeds could have done them better. The credit belongs to the man who is actually in the arena, whose face is marred by dust and sweat and blood; who strives valiantly; who errs and comes short again and again; who knows great enthusiasms, the great devotions; who spends himself in a worthy cause; who at the best, knows in the end the triumph of high achievement, and who, at the worst, if he fails, at least fails while daring greatly so that his place shall never be with those timid souls who neither know victory nor defeat.[1]

Theodore Roosevelt is right. Many people try to tell God why they cannot carry out their divine mission. They say things like, "I'm too old . . . too young . . . too dumb . . . too ugly . . . too uneducated . . . too weird . . . too weak. I was born into the wrong family. I was a prostitute . . . a thief . . . a murderer . . . an adulteress. I've been divorced. I've had an abortion . . . had several." The list goes on and on.

Take courage, folks. If you have made such a list, you are in great company. Life is filled with history makers like us. If you think you are too dumb, remember Samson (see Judges 13–16). That guy was dumb. I mean, when your girlfriend ties you up three times and tells you that your enemy is after you, and you *still* spill the beans, that is an IQ crisis. Yet in the end, Samson's greatest victory followed his greatest defeat.

Perhaps you think you are too young to make a difference. At eight years old, Josiah was too young to cross the street by himself, much less become king. And talk about generational curses—Josiah's grandfather was Manasseh, the most wicked king in Israel's history, and his father was Amon, who walked in all the ways of Manasseh. Yikes! Yet Josiah led Judah into one of its greatest revivals and brought his whole nation back to God (see 2 Kings 22–23).

Maybe you are just plain strange. Join the exalted ranks of John the Baptist. The man was weird. He wore an outfit that never was nor ever has been in style. He ate locusts. You cannot even order those things at the finest restaurants. Yet Jesus said no one greater than John had ever been born.

You still cannot carry out God's mission for you? Ah, I get it—you have some sexual hang-ups. Tell your troubles to Rahab, the prostitute who helped Joshua conquer the Promised Land and who later wound up as the great-great-great-great-grand-mother of Jesus Christ (see Joshua 2; 6; Matthew 1:5).

So you are an ex-con? How about the "man after God's heart" named David, who committed adultery and then murdered the woman's husband (see 2 Samuel 11)?

Oh, but you have a drinking problem. Noah, who coura-geously obeyed God and partnered with Him to save the entire human race, got so drunk that he took off all his clothes (see Genesis 9:20–21).

You think you are too ugly to make a difference? Have you ever seen a picture of Abraham Lincoln? Now, that dude was ugly. He was so ugly that a ten-year-old girl who met him on the campaign trail said, "Mister Lincoln, you're so ugly that you should grow a beard to cover up your face." So he did. Yet that ugly man became one of America's greatest presidents and saved our nation from the tyranny of slavery.

Maybe you have some emotional challenges. Winston Churchill (who looked like Mister Peabody, by the way) had what he called his "black dog." The "dog" was his struggle with depression, which kept him in bed for up to thirty days at a time. Many historians believe Churchill was mentally ill. If so, he did more while mentally ill than most people do in their healthy state of mind.

So you never finished high school? Peter's claim to fame was that since his messages were profound, they had to be from God—because the guy had no education (see Acts 4:13).

The stories go on and on, both in the pages of Scripture and ever since. What is your excuse for not fulfilling your call? Get over it! God is famous for accomplishing extraordinary things with ordinary people.

Braveheart

Many people who call themselves leaders are actually just puppets of the masses. Popular opinion is pulling their strings as they search for the path of least resistance. Their goal is to make decisions that please as many people as possible. What they refuse to understand is that when you fear the people, you are not leading them; they are leading you.

It is important to realize that the organizations we are called to lead can become idols, something we bow down to instead of serve and lead. Dimensions Ministries president and author Jack Taylor put it this way: "An idol is something you have to check with before you say yes to God." It is so easy to find ourselves bowing to the will of the crowd instead of following the cloud of God's direction.

In the movie *Braveheart*, William Wallace tries to convince Robert the Bruce to join his tattered army of makeshift soldiers in freeing Scotland from the tyranny of the English. Bruce argues with Wallace and tries to persuade him to calm down. Finally, Wallace storms out of the castle in a rage, but Robert the Bruce is still in pursuit, trying to convince him to compromise with his enemies and make peace with England. Wallace stops abruptly on the castle steps and turns to Robert the Bruce. The camera zooms in on the two men as they stand there, staring into each other's eyes, for what seems like an eternity. Then, in his best Scottish accent, Wallace delivers the most powerful lines of the entire movie: "Men don't follow titles, they follow courage! If you lead them, they will follow you. It's true, you know. I can see it in your eyes!"

I understand this is just a line in a movie, but it is still true. In this hour, when the political spirit seems to reign supreme and the media's high priesthood crucifies anyone who disagrees with the crowd, God is still searching for a man, for a woman, for somebody who has the courage to stand with Him. He just needs a person who will truly lead, make the call and lift up a cry for righteousness—someone who will be a voice for the Kingdom, not just an echo of past religious ideologies or some political clone or a chameleon whose convictions change with the company he or she keeps.

John Maxwell, the well-known author of many books on leadership, said in his book *Developing the Leader within You* (Thomas Nelson, 2005), "When the leader lacks confidence, the followers lack commitment." Courage inspires people. It is the bridge between what is and what should be.

Dying to Live

Until we have something to die for, we really never live. Jesus put it best: "For whoever wishes to save his life will lose it; but whoever loses his life for My sake will find it" (Matthew 16:25). Everyone's life is terminal. We are all going to die; we just don't know when. The real question is, will we really ever live?

I am not talking about taking up space and sucking up air; I mean really living, making a difference, pushing past our fear and taking hold of our destiny. Until we deal with death, we don't really ever live. The writer of Hebrews put it this way:

> Therefore, since the children share in flesh and blood, He Himself likewise also partook of the same, that through death He might render powerless him who had the power of death, that is, the devil, and might free those who through fear of death were subject to slavery all their lives.
>
> Hebrews 2:14–15

It is only when we deal with the inevitable that we can actually do the impossible. When a person loses the fear of death, he or she begins to move into new realms of impact.

According to an ancient Roman adage, *A coward dies a thousand deaths, but a brave man dies only once!* Fear will rob us of life every day. The life we were called to live lies on the other side of our fears. Remember, God did not childproof the Garden. He is not as interested in keeping us safe as He is in trying to keep us from a meaningless life. Courage is a catalyst to great leadership and a life full of purpose.

Courageous Love

In September 2005, a couple of young people came to Bethel's ministry school. Kerstin was from Switzerland, and Tyson was an American. They fell in love, and it was not long before they were married. They so adored each other that watching them interact was like imagining a scene out of a romantic novel. Soon Kerstin was pregnant with their first child, and their life took on an ecstatic joy that I have rarely ever observed. That same year, Kerstin won our school's highest honor, the M. Earl Johnson Award, which is only given to two students per class for their outstanding character, achievement and anointing.

Kerstin and Tyson were on top of the world, and we were all being pulled along in the wake of their elation.

Then suddenly, something terrible happened. Early in Kerstin's pregnancy, she returned from the doctor with a serious report of stage 4 cancer that had spread through most of her body. She was rushed to a specialist, who confirmed her condition. The doctors felt confident that they could save her life if she began treatment immediately, but they explained that the chemotherapy would likely kill the baby.

The choice was clear—either abort the baby and live, or carry the child to full term and die. Kerstin did not hesitate; her mind was made up. She would give up her life to save her child, if necessary. Five months later, a healthy baby boy named Kalani came into the world to two very excited parents. Kalani means "heavenly," and he was certainly a gift from God. In the meantime, our church prayed, fasted and warred over Kerstin's condition. But eight months after this heavenly child was born, his earthly mother was gone.

Most people spend their existence trying to save their life, wondering why they are never really fulfilled. Maybe Mick Jagger said it best when he sang his song titled "(I Can't Get No) Satisfaction."[2] But Kerstin had the courage to lay down her life so that someone else would live. Do you?

Alexander the Great

This courage to die for something has always been a vital ingredient in any history-making endeavor. Alexander the Great is a classic example of a leader who inspired people to give their lives for something greater than themselves. A few centuries before Christ, Alexander conquered most of the known world with his military strength. One day, Alexander and a small company of soldiers approached a strongly defended, walled city. Standing outside the walls, Alexander raised his voice and demanded to see the king. Standing on the battlements above the invading army, the king agreed to hear Alexander's demands.

"Surrender to me immediately," commanded Alexander.

"Why should I surrender to you?" the king laughed. "We have you far outnumbered. You are no threat to us!"

Alexander replied confidently, "Allow me to demonstrate why you should surrender."

Alexander ordered his men to line up single file and start marching. He marched them straight toward a sheer cliff that dropped hundreds of feet to the rocks below. The king and his soldiers watched in shocked disbelief as, one by one, Alexander's soldiers marched without hesitation right off the cliff to their deaths. After ten soldiers had died, Alexander ordered the rest of his men to stop and return to his side. The king and his soldiers surrendered on the spot.

Masquerade

There are so many things in life that masquerade as courage but are really just fear dressed up in a valor costume. When folks make comments like, "I don't care what people think of me," they are deceiving themselves. Everybody needs affection and encouragement from others. It is just human nature. The real issue with these people is that they are afraid that if others get to know them, they will not like them. They work hard, therefore, to reject others before others have a chance to reject them.

Then there are the "I do all the talking" folks who live in fear. Have you ever had a conversation with someone who refuses to let you get a word in edgewise? These people are terrified of being controlled by others, so they will not let anyone speak into their lives.

How about the rageaholic? He stays mad so he does not have to feel fearful.

Then there is the seductive woman or the beauty queen who is frightened by men and has learned how to use her body to reduce aggressive lions to purring pussycats.

Then there is the brainiac who needs to be smarter than everyone else to deal with his insecurities. He believes that as long as he can outthink everyone on the planet, he will not have to be afraid of them.

Then there is the bodybuilder who may be using another fear crutch, dealing with his or her trepidation by being stronger than everyone else.

Or have you ever met the Bible scholar guy? He knows everything about the Book and hides behind religion.

The list could go on and on. I am not suggesting in any way that beauty, brains, talent or muscles are wrong in themselves (rage is an exception, of course). But when we are motivated by fear instead of inspired by faith, the wrong spirit anoints our strengths.

Courageous Types

There are two types of courage that are admired in the Kingdom of God. The first one I call the "fear that has said its prayers" kind of courage. It is courage that takes action in the midst of intense fear. Esther demonstrated this class of courage. Haman, the king's right-hand man, hated a Jewish man named Mordecai because he refused to treat him like a god. In revenge, Haman—not knowing that the queen herself was Jewish—convinced the king to exterminate all the Jews.

Mordecai was Queen Esther's cousin and was responsible for her becoming queen in the first place. He discovered Haman's genocidal plot, dressed himself in sackcloth, and arrived mourning and wailing at the king's gate.

Troubled and scared, Esther tried to calm him down and get him to change his clothes. This is where the plot thickens. Mordecai brought Esther to the point of action with these famous words:

> Do not imagine that you in the king's palace can escape any more than all the Jews. For if you remain silent at this time, relief and deliverance will arise for the Jews from another place and you and your father's house will perish. And who knows whether you have not attained royalty for such a time as this?
>
> Esther 4:13–14

After this, Esther sent a message in reply to Mordecai. She instructed him,

> Go, assemble all the Jews who are found in Susa, and fast for me; do not eat or drink for three days, night or day. I and my maidens also will fast in the same way. And thus I will go in to the king, which is not according to the law; and if I perish, I perish.
>
> Esther 4:16

Queen Esther was stressed out, but she refused to let her fear dictate her future. She entered the palace and appealed to her king. She won the king's favor, and he hung Haman on the very gallows that Haman had erected for Mordecai. Esther rescued the Jews and saved the day.

The dogs of doom often stand at the doors of our destiny. They start barking when we are about to cross the threshold of our God-given purpose. Most people never fully enter into their promised land because they allow fear to dictate the boundaries of their future. They reduce their lives to accommodate the dogs of doom, and they mistake the silence for peace.

For example, if you are so afraid to fly that you never get on a plane, you will not feel scared. But you have scaled back your life to silence the dogs. You may think you are absolutely tranquil, but the truth is that you are still full of fear. Subconsciously, you know that flying will awaken the sleeping monster, and he will torment you until you slay him or obey him.

Slaying Dragons

These fear dragons have wandered the earth and tormented people for generations. It was these same fearmongers who, thousands of years ago, kept the children of Israel out of the land God had promised them. There are always giants waiting for us at the border of our destiny, because we need them. The process of conquering them is what prepares us to prosper in the Promised Land. It is fear-and-trembling courage that moves us past the Goliaths of our life.

The great apostle Paul, who courageously endured imprisonment, stoning, beatings and shipwreck, was left for dead on at least one occasion and was finally beheaded. He told the Corinthians, "I was with you in weakness and in fear and in much trembling" (1 Corinthians 2:3). Later he wrote these words to the believers at Philippi:

> So then, my beloved, just as you have always obeyed, not as in my presence only, but now much more in my absence, work out your salvation with fear and trembling; for it is God who is at work in you, both to will and to work for His good pleasure.
>
> Philippians 2:12–13

We see clearly through the life of Paul that courage does not necessarily mean you are not afraid. Most often, bravery is actually demonstrated in the face of fear. It is only in facing our fears that we can conquer them and capture our destiny.

Many people are under the illusion that brave people are somehow immune to anxiety. This simply is not true. Fear is a human emotion common to everyone. Luke described Jesus' emotional state hours before He was crucified by saying that Jesus was in agony to the point where He was sweating drops of blood (see Luke 22:44). I would say that this was a manifestation of pretty intense fear. Courage is not an emotional state, but rather the choice we make to overcome our feelings so that we can obtain our desired outcome.

There is another type of courage that we also see demonstrated throughout the Bible. I am talking about unreasonable, supernatural courage that transcends the mind, will and emotions. Acts 4 and 5 give us a perfect example of supernatural courage:

> And when they had summoned them, they commanded them not to speak or teach at all in the name of Jesus. But Peter and John answered and said to them, "Whether it is right in the sight of God to give heed to you rather than to God, you be the judge; for we cannot stop speaking about what we have seen and heard." When they had threatened them further, they let them go (finding no basis on which to punish them). . . .
>
> When they had been released, they went to their own companions and reported all that the chief priests and the elders had said to them. And when they heard this, they lifted their voices to God with one accord and said, "O Lord, it is You who made the heavens and the earth and the sea, and all that is in them, who by the Holy Spirit, through the mouth of our father David Your servant, said,
>
>> 'Why did the Gentiles rage,
>> And the peoples devise futile things?
>> The kings of the earth took their stand,
>> and the rulers were gathered together
>> Against the LORD and against His Christ.'
>
> For truly in this city there were gathered together against Your holy servant Jesus, whom You anointed, both Herod and Pontius Pilate, along with the Gentiles and the peoples of Israel, to do whatever Your hand and Your purpose predestined to occur.

And now, Lord, take note of their threats, and grant that *Your bond-servants may speak Your word with all confidence,* while You extend Your hand to heal, and signs and wonders take place through the name of Your holy servant Jesus." And when they had prayed, the place where they had gathered together was shaken, and they were all filled with the Holy Spirit and began to speak the word of God with boldness.

Acts 4:18–21, 23–31, emphasis added

And after calling the apostles in, they flogged them and ordered them not to speak in the name of Jesus, and then released them. So they went on their way from the presence of the Council, rejoicing that they had been considered worthy to suffer shame for His name. And every day, in the temple and from house to house, they kept right on teaching and preaching Jesus as the Christ.

Acts 5:40–42

We cannot psych ourselves up into supernatural courage. It is a divine boldness that only the Lord Himself can impart to us. When we receive this gift of courage, as the apostles did in these passages, we feel as though there is an invisible force field protecting us.

My Story

I have experienced this kind of courage on many occasions. One of the more dramatic times occurred in the summer of 1994. Kathy and I took our son's eighth-grade class, consisting of eight kids, to Santa Cruz Beach to celebrate their graduation. We headed for home at dusk in a borrowed fifteen-passenger van.

A couple of hours into our homeward journey, the kids wanted to stop so they could use the restroom. We pulled off the freeway and stopped at a convenience store. The kids piled out, went to the bathroom, grabbed something to eat and piled back in. As we entered the freeway on-ramp, I noticed in my rearview mirror an old white Chevy pickup truck tailgating us. I probably would not have thought much about it, except that I heard a voice in my spirit say, *Peace be with you. No harm shall come to any of you.*

What a strange thing to hear, I thought as an intense, overwhelming peace came over me. It felt as if I had jumped into an ocean of courage.

After we entered the freeway, the tailgating truck pulled alongside us. The driver rolled down his passenger window and started shouting and motioning to me to pull over. I slowed the van and began to exit onto the shoulder of the road, still trying to interpret the man's concerns. By now, his yelling and motioning had grown more intense. I lowered my window and further reduced my speed as he pulled within inches of the van. I thought I could hear him say that our rear tire was flat, so I came to a stop.

The Chevy truck stopped right next to us, its driver seemingly oblivious to the fact that his truck was blocking one lane of the freeway. He continued yelling something, but I could not understand a word he was saying. Then something crazy happened. I looked into his eyes, and they were *glowing red*. I don't mean that he had pinkeye or looked tired—I mean his eyes were *glowing*. Then I heard a small voice inside me say, *Get out of here!*

I shouted "thank you" to the man and began to maneuver my way back onto the freeway. As I did, the man's mood turned to rage and he ran us off the road, boxing us in against the freeway fence. Then he jumped out of the truck. I now saw that he was a white man in his early thirties, wearing a ragged T-shirt and dirty jeans. He began to run toward the passenger door of our van.

One of the kids screamed, "He has a gun!"

I threw the van into drive and floored it, narrowly squeezing between the fence and his truck. As I cleared the Chevy, I glanced into my rearview mirror and saw the guy running for his vehicle. I stepped on it, hoping to lose him quickly and exit the freeway. But within seconds he was right on our tail, trying to ram us from behind.

The kids started freaking out, yelling, "He's going to ram us! He's trying to hit us from behind!"

I smashed the accelerator to the floor and our speed increased to 80, then 90, then 100 miles per hour. But the old truck stayed within inches of our bumper.

Meanwhile, fear had overwhelmed almost everybody in the van. Kathy and the kids were shouting and crying. Kathy became hysterical and began pleading with me to pull over. But an amazing peace kept washing over me like warm water. The peace was so intense that I found myself laughing through much of the ordeal. I don't think anyone else saw the humor in it at all, especially my wife.

The crazy guy continued to try to slam into us. I veered from lane to lane, using the entire freeway to avoid a collision. The other cars on the road began to slow down and give us room to maneuver as they observed the assault. I could not lose the guy, so about forty miles into the chase I decided to pull over and see what he would do with so many witnesses watching him. I came to a complete stop on the right shoulder of the road. Traffic in both directions came to a halt.

To my surprise, the man pulled into the median and turned his truck sideways. Then he headed right for us at full speed and tried to crash into us from the side. I stepped on the gas, narrowly escaping his attack. He crashed into the freeway fence, and his truck got stuck in the deep gravel shoulder.

I jumped on the accelerator, and our large van roared to speeds of over 110 miles per hour. Cars on the road pulled over to let us through as we tried to race to safety. Several minutes passed, and then suddenly, as if from nowhere, the white Chevy truck appeared in my rearview mirror again. Within seconds he managed to get alongside us.

I swerved back and forth over the entire road, even using the gravel shoulders on both sides of the freeway to escape his assault. Several times, I sped up to 100 miles per hour and then slammed on the brakes, swerving just as he was about to ram us from behind and forcing him to pass us. Then I would drive hard to stay behind him.

Finally, we passed a highway patrolman who had someone pulled over on the right shoulder of the road. I slammed on the brakes and pulled into the median. The madman pulled in front of me and tried to sideswipe me as he skidded to a stop. I jammed it into reverse and floored it, desperately trying to get back near the patrol car. At last the officer came into our sights.

Kathy rolled down her window and began shouting hysterically to the officer, "He's trying to kill us! Please help us! He's trying to kill us!"

I came to a stop in the median. There were just three lanes separating us from the officer. I tried to wait there as Kathy continued struggling to get the cop's attention. It was starting to get dark by now, and I knew the crazy guy was near, but I could not figure out where he had stopped.

All of a sudden, the back door of the van opened and the girls in the backseat starting screaming, "He's gotten in the back door! He's getting in the van!" Reaching over the seat, the girls managed to hold the door partway closed.

"Hold on!" I shouted.

I forced the shifter into drive and jumped on it, throwing the man to the ground. I wanted to stay close to the patrolman, so I stopped once more, hoping he would see us. But the nutcase who was chasing us jumped up on the running boards, forced the window open and managed to unlock the side door.

Jason and Andy were restraining a boy on the floor who was screaming and trying to escape. Jason reached up with one hand, grasped the door handle and struggled to hold the door closed, yelling, "Dad, he's getting in the side door!"

"Hang on!" I shouted back. I dropped it in reverse and floored the accelerator. Again the perpetrator fell off the van. I began speeding forward and backward to keep him out of the van, still trying to remain in the view of the officer.

All at once, I heard someone outside the van yell, "Stop, or I'll blow your head off!"

Good, I thought, *the cops finally got him*. But when I turned and looked ahead, I saw that the highway patrolman had his gun pointed right at my head, just inches from the windshield.

"Out of the van!" he commanded.

I slowly unbuckled my seatbelt and opened the door. He put his gun in my chest and threw me to the ground.

"You have the wrong guy!" I pleaded with him. "Dude, you're arresting the wrong man!"

The officer cuffed me from behind and dragged me to the passenger's side of the van. I saw then that the crazy guy was lying on the ground in handcuffs also. Within seconds, highway patrol cars, police cars and a helicopter encircled us.

Even in cuffs, incredible peace continued to flow over me. I overheard the crazy guy telling the police that I had kidnapped his daughter. The officers lined our girls up against the van and asked him to identify his daughter. When he could not find her, they hauled him off in the patrol car. When the story was finally straight, they released me and we drove home without further incident.

At six o'clock the next morning, the phone rang. Startled and groggy, I picked it up. "Hello," I grunted.

There was a long pause, but I could hear someone quietly weeping on the other end. "Hello," I said, a little more cheerfully this time.

"Hi, I'm the officer who arrested you last night." Choking back tears, he continued, "I want to apologize to you for treating you that way." Unable to disguise his weeping, he went on, "When your wife said, 'He's trying to kill us' and the man said you kidnapped his daughter, I thought you were the assailant. When you wouldn't stop the van, I decided to shoot you to save the family. But as I aimed my gun and squeezed the trigger, something said, *Don't shoot!* I've been on the force for twenty years and have never pulled my gun on anyone. I almost killed you!"

"Oh, don't worry about it," I answered. "I'm a Christian and the Lord told me when it all started, *Peace be with you*, and, *No harm shall come to any of you.* So you couldn't have shot me."

Apparently shocked and still crying, the officer hung up.

Most of the eighth-grade class was powerfully moved by God's divine protection. Many of them got up in front of the church on Sunday morning and shared how much the trip had impacted them. The story of God's supernatural protection circulated through our small town for many years.

If we are going to transform cities, disciple nations and see heaven literally come to earth, it is going to take true valor—supernatural courage that defies the intelligent, confronts the political spirit and forces the dogs of doom to back down. It is time for us to ask heaven for an infusion of boldness that possesses our souls and inspires our spirits.

12

:::

The Land of the Giants

Excellence is the result of caring more than others think
is wise, risking more than others think is safe, dreaming
more than others think is practical, and expecting more
than others think is possible.

Ronnie Max Oldham

I t was a warm summer afternoon in Australia. About two hundred leaders had gathered for a leadership conference where
I was teaching on the subject of greatness. I wanted to use
some examples that my audience could relate to in order to
emphasize the fact that it is heroes who make history.

I was unfamiliar with Australia's past, so I asked the crowd,
"Who are the heroes in your nation?"

They were completely silent.

After a few moments of increasing tension, I pressed, "Come
on, Aussies, who are the most famous people in Australia? You

know what I mean. The United States has George Washington, Abraham Lincoln and Billy Graham. England has Winston Churchill, and South Africa has Nelson Mandela. Who are the heroes of this country?"

The hush continued in the room. Finally, the senior leader on the front row broke the silence.

"Kris," he whispered, obviously trying not to embarrass me, "we don't have heroes in our nation. It's culturally taboo to be great in Australia. It's called the tall poppy syndrome."

After the meeting ended, some of the pastoral team came over and explained to me that the tall poppy syndrome is a social dynamic in which anyone who accomplishes something outstanding or somehow stands above the crowd is cut down by the masses.

I was stunned to learn that this was a guiding principle in their culture, and I wondered if they understood that this social dynamic inherently leads people to resist advancement, innovation or progress. As I pondered the Australian mindset, however, it occurred to me that much of the Body of Christ has an identical culture. Plenty of churches are teaching people how to be *good*, but few are inspiring people to *greatness*.

Humility and Greatness

False humility is largely to blame for the Church's tall poppy syndrome. In my first book, *The Supernatural Ways of Royalty*, I investigated the true nature of humility. I want to review briefly one biblical example that demonstrates how true humility is entirely compatible with confidence, strength and every other aspect of greatness.

The fourth chapter of Daniel records the testimony of King Nebuchadnezzar, who had a dream about a huge tree that covered the earth and became shade for the animals, birds and creatures of the planet. In the midst of this amazing vision, the king heard a voice shout,

> Chop down the tree and cut off its branches, strip off its foliage and scatter its fruit; let the beasts flee from under it and the birds from its branches. Yet leave the stump with its roots in the ground, but with a band of iron and bronze around it in the new grass of the field; and let him be drenched with the dew of heaven, and let him share with the beasts in the grass of the earth. Let his mind be changed from that of a man and let a beast's mind be given to him, and let seven periods of time pass over him.
>
> Daniel 4:14–16

The king was understandably freaked out by the dream and called in his top spiritual consultants to interpret it. Just as the magicians, conjurers and diviners were telling the king that they could not translate the dream, Daniel walked into the room. (You have to love this guy's timing; he always seemed to be just a little late everywhere he went.) Nebuchadnezzar related the dream to Daniel, who immediately received the interpretation from God.

What Daniel did next may be a little off the subject of humility, but it is still worth commenting on. Before he explained the meaning of the dream, Daniel said to the king, "My lord, if only the dream applied to those who hate you and its interpretation to your adversaries!" (Daniel 4:19). Daniel truly loved the kings he served, in spite of the fact that they destroyed his country, probably killed his family, and took him captive to serve at their will. Nebuchadnezzar was so wicked, but there is a powerful lesson embedded in this story. If we are ever going to be invited into the palace to advise kings and mentor nations, we had better figure out how to love our enemies and help leaders with whom we don't agree.

Daniel explained that the tree the angel chopped down in the dream actually represented Nebuchadnezzar. Apparently, the king's destructive behavior, arrogance and pride had finally gotten him in hot water with God, and the Lord of heaven was about to discipline him severely. Daniel went on to counsel Nebuchadnezzar, advising that he try to avoid this calamity by humbling himself. But the hardheaded king did not listen, and a year later his world came crashing in on him. Here is the account of his demise:

> Twelve months later he was walking on the roof of the royal palace of Babylon. The king reflected and said, "Is this not Babylon the great, which I myself have built as a royal residence by the might of my power and for the glory of my majesty?" While the word was in the king's mouth, a voice came from heaven, saying, "King Nebuchadnezzar, to you it is declared: sovereignty has been removed from you, and you will be driven away from mankind, and your dwelling place will be with the beasts of the field. You will be given grass to eat like cattle, and seven periods of time will pass over you until you recognize that the Most High is ruler over the realm of mankind and bestows it on whomever He wishes." Immediately the word concerning Nebuchadnezzar was fulfilled; and he was driven away from mankind and began eating grass like cattle, and his body was drenched with the dew of heaven until his hair had grown like eagles' feathers and his nails like birds' claws.

> Daniel 4:29–33

The insane king lived in exile for seven years. Finally, that terrible season came to an end and God restored him. Evidently, Nebuchadnezzar kept a journal of his restoration. His thoughts and reflections became part of the book of Daniel. King Nebuchadnezzar wrote,

> At that time my reason returned to me. And my majesty and splendor were restored to me for the glory of my kingdom, and

my counselors and my nobles began seeking me out; so I was reestablished in my sovereignty, and surpassing greatness was added to me. Now I, Nebuchadnezzar, praise, exalt and honor the King of heaven, for all His works are true and His ways just, and He is able to humble those who walk in pride.

Daniel 4:36–37

God removed this king because of his arrogance and self-absorbed lifestyle. But when the Almighty restored Nebuchadnezzar's mind, the king said *humbly* that his *majesty, splendor, glory, sovereignty and surpassing greatness* were restored to him. The obvious point here is that humility is not feeling bad about yourself or thinking you are little, insignificant or anything else demeaning. True humility begins with remembering the source of your greatness, the King of heaven. The truth of God's grace humbles a man without degrading him and exalts a man without inflating him.

Being Exalted

Humility is not only compatible with greatness; it is the process of significance. We see this clearly in Jesus' statement "Whoever exalts himself shall be humbled; and whoever humbles himself shall be exalted" (Matthew 23:12). According to Christ, the act of humility is the pathway to promotion. Jesus was not criticizing the desire for greatness; He was *encouraging* it by showing us how to attain it.

Hopefully, we all agree that Jesus is the model of humility, as He is of all other things. If this is true, then we only need to ask ourselves one simple question: What happened when Jesus humbled Himself? Paul tells us:

[Jesus] emptied Himself, taking the form of a bond-servant, and being made in the likeness of men. . . . For this reason also, *God highly exalted Him*, and bestowed on Him the name which is above every name, so that at the name of Jesus every knee will bow, of those who are in heaven and on earth and under the earth, and that every tongue will confess that Jesus Christ is Lord, to the glory of God the Father.

Philippians 2:7, 9–11, emphasis added

Just in case you were wondering, being exalted means being *raised high*. In the Kingdom, humility is designed to make us "tall poppies." Yet so often in the Church, we have emphasized the process while demeaning the promise, which in turn creates frustration and confusion. We must remove this contradiction from our core values and begin to allow those who submit to the process Jesus modeled to receive its intended reward. Here are fifteen true attributes of humility that must remain in our lives as God exalts us:

1. We must remain teachable.
2. We have to be influenceable.
3. We have to be able to receive correction without defending ourselves.
4. We must rejoice when others are celebrated.
5. No job can be too small for us.
6. We don't always have to be right.
7. We should naturally seek the advice of others.
8. We actually do pray and not just talk about it.
9. We must freely admit our flaws, mistakes and failures.
10. We have to live to help others succeed.
11. We cannot be easily offended.
12. We have to have a thankful attitude.
13. We must refuse to live with a sense of entitlement, thinking someone owes us something.

14. We have to be quick to forgive and not hold grudges.
15. We have to be confident in who we are and content with who we are not.

A House of Heroes

I cannot help but notice that all twelve of the men who hung out with Jesus, although they came from different occupations and backgrounds, eventually had one thing in common. They all thought they were supposed to be great. There is something about the presence of Jesus that causes people to dream of prominence, grandeur and greatness. If we are going to see a reformation in the Church that translates into true global transformation, we are going to have to cultivate, encourage and embrace a house of heroes.

It was King David who originally established the "house of the mighty men" (see Nehemiah 3:16). Like Jesus after him, David had a way of turning weaklings into warriors. (Can you imagine a house where the mighty men of David lived together? That is what I would call a neighborhood watch!) David's mighty men lived together in the same house, which allowed them to establish and sustain a heroic culture. You can bet there was no such thing as the tall poppy syndrome in David's house of heroes.

If the Church is going to become a place where mighty men and women can be trained, equipped and deployed, then we need leaders who are like Jesus and David. As I discussed in *The Supernatural Ways of Royalty*, the primary reason false humility persists in the Church is that we still don't really know who we are in God. We need confident fathers to be restored to the Body of Christ to reestablish the royal identity of the people of God. Jesus' supreme confidence in His identity as the Son of God enabled Him to call out sonship in His disciples.

David's kingly identity, which he embraced long before he ever sat on a throne, caused him to turn a band of rejects into a company of royal warriors. If we are going to develop a culture that deploys world changers, our leaders must first be established in their own identity in God. We need Jesus to hang out with us in such a way that we become possessed by the same sense of royal identity and epic vision that His disciples experienced in the days when He walked this planet.

Absent or Empowering

Lots of leaders think they are empowering their people, when actually as leaders they are just absent. Empowering others and being absent from them are not the same thing. A father who rarely comes home would never be mistaken for being an empowering presence in his household. Leaders who hardly ever come out of their office or who seldom interact with their teams are like a father or mother who never comes home. They may think they are being empowering by removing the negative element of control from the culture, but people don't necessarily feel powerful just because nobody is resisting them. More often than not, their leader's absence leaves them feeling lost, abandoned and unsure of what they are supposed to be doing. Empowering leaders have a proactive, not inactive, ability. They do not simply remove the controlling dynamics; they establish positive elements of communication, encouragement, direction, praise and cooperation.

Incidentally, absent leaders can be just as controlling as the ones who get into everybody's business. We most often think of controlling leaders as micromanagers or angry people who rule through fear and intimidation. Actually, one of the most common ways to control people is to withdraw and withhold information. But Jesus equated withholding information with slavery. He put it this way: "No longer do I call you slaves, for the slave does not know what his master is doing; but I have called you friends, for all things that I have heard from My Father I have made known to you" (John 15:15).

You can find a great example of how withholding information enslaves people in the Genesis story of Joseph and the famine. Joseph interpreted Pharaoh's dreams as being about seven years of plenty, followed by seven years of famine. Then he wisely instructed Pharaoh to store 20 percent of all of the grain in Egypt during the seven years of abundance so there would be enough food to feed the nation during the famine (see Genesis 41). But Joseph withheld the revelation about the coming famine from the Egyptian population, as well as withholding his plan to store food. The result was that all of Egypt's inhabitants became slaves as they sold themselves to Pharaoh for food:

> "Why should we die before your eyes, both we and our land? Buy us and our land for food, and we and our land will be slaves to Pharaoh. So give us seed, that we may live and not die, and that the land may not be desolate."
>
> So Joseph bought all the land of Egypt for Pharaoh, for every Egyptian sold his field, because the famine was severe upon them. Thus the land became Pharaoh's.
>
> Genesis 47:19–20

If Joseph simply had shared with all the people the same revelation he had given to Pharaoh, the Egyptians would have become the richest people on the planet, because the famine had affected the entire known world and people were coming from every nation to purchase food. Instead, Joseph's secret created a two-class system (rich and poor), and a first-world nation became a third-world nation in one generation. Symptomatic cures become tomorrow's problems, and it is important to understand what kind of ecosystem our decisions will create for future generations. The next pharaoh who rose to power enslaved the Israelites (see Exodus 1).

Empowering leaders make decisions *with* people, not just *for* people. When we withhold information from our people or tell them only what they need to know to get their jobs done, we produce slave camps in which one person does all the thinking. This is religion on steroids. Religion wants to tame people, domesticate the masses and get them to keep the rules. But new ideas are never discovered behind the iron bars of the zoo. It is only in the uncharted jungle of life that new realities and opportunities are revealed. If we are going to become a house of heroes, we need fresh ideas, untried solutions, innovation and bold, courageous thoughts delivered by risk takers, not zookeepers.

In His friendship with His disciples, Jesus did not merely tell them *what* to think; He taught them through His conversations and interactions with them *how* to think. He did not keep them on the sidelines, watching Him do everything. They had permission to ask questions, try to do what He was doing and get His feedback. More than that, Jesus told them to do even greater things than He did. True Kingdom-minded fathers and mothers want their sons and daughters to succeed them and exceed them.

Living for the Reward

We will never nurture greatness in people without cultivating a culture of reward. I would like to propose to you that no truly great feat has ever been accomplished without (at least in part) the promise of reward. For example, David killed Goliath so that he could marry the king's daughter (see 1 Samuel 17:25). The Israelites left Egypt to obtain a Promised Land (see Exodus 3:8, 17). Jesus Himself achieved His greatest victory for the sake of reward: "For the joy set before Him He endured the cross" (Hebrews 12:2). History books are full of stories about godly people who accomplished great things *for the sake of reward.*

But *reward* has become a dirty word in many religious circles. Some have deemed it unspiritual even to think of rewarding people for their efforts. If you were a carpenter, a mechanic or were employed in any other occupation, it would never dawn on you to do your job and have your employer decide how much to pay you after you were done with the work. Yet if you are a conference speaker in some Christian circles, you had better not act as if you even care about how much the offering is! If you require a certain dollar amount per session when you speak at conferences, you most likely will be tagged as a materialist. (Don't worry; I never ask for an offering when I speak, and I am well taken care of.)

Neither am I advocating that we should work for money instead of working for God. But I am saying that God intends that the thought of a reward in working for Him would motivate us as surely as does the thought of payment from our employers. The fact that we struggle over things like paying spiritual leaders a wage for their labors indicates that we don't truly understand God's heavenly economy. It is spiritual to expect God to compensate us for our efforts. Jesus said, "The laborer is worthy of his wages" (Luke 10:7). The gospels' parables of the ten talents, the ten minas and the sower are all about working for a reward. And the last chapter of the Good Book says, "Behold, I am coming quickly, and My *reward* is with Me, to render to every man according to what he has done" (Revelation 22:12, emphasis added).

Reward is the driving motivation of our *faith.* The writer of Hebrews says, "Without faith it is impossible to please Him, for he who comes to God must believe that He is and that He is a rewarder of those who seek Him" (Hebrews 11:6). When people argue that as a Christian you should not care about reward, it is like saying that you should not believe in God. You simply cannot please God unless you expect Him to reward you.

One of the main ways we create a culture of reward is by celebrating people's accomplishments. Of course, it is no surprise that folks who struggle with the idea of reward also resist compliments, praise or being acknowledged for their achievements. I have been to churches where they don't even clap when the worship band rocks. In some circles, celebrating people's efforts is seen as unspiritual, self-promoting or arrogant. Many people actually believe that recognizing a person's success steals glory from God. But isn't it God who created us and gave each of us special gifts and abilities? We cheer for our kids when they are playing sports. We never think, *That kid is stealing my glory!*

Actually, when one of my kids did something amazing on the court or on the field, I would turn to the other parents and say, "Whose kid is that?"

Everyone would laugh and say, "We know it's yours!"

The truth is that when we do something awesome on the earth, God is the loudest one in the stands of life, cheering us on. He's saying things like, "*Whose* son is that? That kid takes after his Daddy! That girl is amazing!"

The great exploits of God's sons and daughters actually glorify the Father. That is why Paul wrote, "Therefore be imitators of God, as beloved children" (Ephesians 5:1). When we imitate God, we are being ourselves. We were created in His image, and we are commanded to become Christlike. There is nothing too noble to reach for, too awesome to believe for, too powerful to hope for or too excellent to live for . . . because we are children of the *King*.

Serial Killers

Jealousy is the evil adversary of greatness. It begins as a selfish sin, but it acts like a watchman who deliberately dislodges the royal gates, allowing a vicious enemy access. Jealousy is a serial killer. The apostle James warns us that what is initiated as a struggle in our hearts eventually gives place to demonic spirits that wreak havoc on the very core of our being:

> But if you have bitter jealousy and selfish ambition in your heart, do not be arrogant and *so* lie against the truth. This wisdom is not that which comes down from above, but is *earthly, natural, demonic. For where jealousy and selfish ambition exist*, there is disorder and *every evil thing*.
>
> James 3:14–16, emphasis added

The account of Saul and David returning from the most famous battle in Jewish history illustrates this point so well:

> It happened as they were coming, when David returned from killing the Philistine, that the women came out of all the cities of Israel, singing and dancing, to meet King Saul, with tambourines, with joy and with musical instruments. The women sang as they played, and said,
>
> > "Saul has slain his thousands,
> > And David his ten thousands."
>
> Then Saul became very angry, for this saying displeased him; and he said, "They have ascribed to David ten thousands, but to me they have ascribed thousands. Now what more can he have but the kingdom?" *Saul looked at David with suspicion [jealousy] from that day on.*
> Now it came about on the next day that *an evil spirit from God came mightily upon Saul*, and he raved in the midst of the house, while David was playing the harp with his hand, as usual; and a

spear was in Saul's hand. Saul hurled the spear for he thought, "I will pin David to the wall." But David escaped from his presence twice.

Now Saul was afraid of David, for the LORD was with him but had departed from Saul.

1 Samuel 18:6–12, emphasis added

David was Saul's spiritual son and he had just killed Goliath, eliminating the greatest threat in Israel's history. It was the presence of giants that kept more than a million people out of the land of God's promises. But instead of King Saul behaving like a father and celebrating his son's victory, he became jealous and suspicious of David. This created an axis of evil in the interior of his soul, attracting evil spirits of insanity and murder that tormented Saul into trying to destroy David.

This pattern is repeated over and over all throughout the Bible. For instance, there was Cain, who murdered his brother Abel because he was jealous of Abel's relationship with God (see Genesis 4). There was Joseph the dreamer, whose brothers hated him because of his grand vision and his father's favor. Their jealousy ultimately drove them to sell Joseph into slavery (see Genesis 37). And who can forget Jesus' disciples, whose envy toward one another kept them in a perpetual state of competition (see Mark 10:35–41; Luke 9:46)?

The tall poppy syndrome is the fruit of leaders who react to these sibling rivalries by changing the structure to eliminate jealousy, instead of dealing with the heart issues. It is interesting to note that Jesus cultivated a culture that potentially fostered jealousy by favoring a few disciples. He took only Peter, James and John with Him to the Mount of Transfiguration (see Mark 9:1–4). When He raised the synagogue official's daughter from the dead, He put everyone out of the room except the same three guys (see Mark 5:37). When Jesus was stressed out before the crucifixion, He only invited Peter, James and John to pray with Him in the Garden of Gethsemane. Although *all* the disciples fought amongst themselves for prominence, Jesus did nothing to dispel their envy of one another, but continued to favor the same three guys. In other words, Jesus refused to change their circumstances to deal with their character issues. His prescription for their jealousy was simple: Humble yourselves by becoming like a child (see Matthew 18:1–4).

We need to understand that our circumstances never *cause* heart issues; they only reveal them. When leaders adjust the conditions of people's circumstances to accommodate their sins, they become peacekeepers (not to be confused with peacemakers) who choose to silence people's complaining instead of allowing the crucible of their state of affairs to purify their hearts. But in a dark corner of the silent sanctuary wall of the soul creeps the poisonous mold of evil. This often goes completely unnoticed until one day the heart is attacked, causing irreversible damage or even death.

Whenever we let sin—and jealousy is sin—dictate our choices, we have already reduced the impact of our movement down to the loudest voice of immaturity in the room. This attitude ultimately derails our God-given destiny.

Pastor Cleddie Keith of Heritage Fellowship in Florence, Kentucky, says, "If you're jealous of someone, invest in them, and then their victory will be your victory." It is paramount that leaders create a culture of reward in which sons and daughters recognize that victories are always a family affair, creating a kind of synergistic amplification that eventually benefits everyone.

Following the Heart of the King

Celebrating the victories of others instead of competing with them creates a "team first" mentality. Teamwork is the result of everyone taking ownership of the corporate mission. John

Maxwell once said, "People support what they help create." The goal of every great leader must be to transfer ownership of the mission to his team, flock or staff. When people take ownership of the corporate call, they need very little oversight, because their souls are possessed by the heart of the King.

This principle is powerfully captured in the story of King Robert the Bruce and his courageous soldiers. Although the movie *Braveheart* depicts William Wallace as the hero of Scotland, the real hero was Robert the Bruce. Wallace won many battles against the English, but it was King Robert who finally freed his nation from the tyranny of the British. Historian Henrietta (H. E.) Marshall tells the story this way:

> King Robert did not live long to enjoy the peace which at last had come to the land. He was not an old man, but he had lived such a hard life that he seemed older than he was. Now he became so ill that he knew he could not live long.
>
> When he felt that he was dying, he called all his nobles and wise men to him. As they stood round him, Bruce told them that he must soon die, and bade them honour his little son David as their King.
>
> With tears of sorrow the nobles promised to do as the King asked.
>
> Bruce then turned to the good Lord James. "My dearest and best friend," he said, "you know how hard I have had to fight for my kingdom. At the time when I was sorest pressed, I made a vow that when God should grant me peace, I should go to the Holy Land to fight for the Sepulchre of Christ. But now that I have peace, my body is feeble, and I cannot fulfil my heart's desire. Yet I would fain send my heart whither my body cannot go. There is no knight so gallant as you, my dear and special friend. Therefore I pray you, when I am dead take my heart from my body, carry it to the Holy Land, and there bury it."
>
> At first Douglas could not speak for tears. After a few minutes he said, "Gallant and noble King, I thank you a thousand times for the honour you do me. Your command shall be obeyed."

"Dear friend, I thank you. You give me your promise?" said the Bruce.

"Most willingly. Upon my knighthood I swear it."

"Thanks be to God. Now I die in peace, since I know that the bravest knight in all my kingdom will do for me what I cannot do for myself," said the King, as he lay back content.

Not many days after this the great King died. From all the land there arose a cry of mourning and sorrow. With tears and sobs, with the sound of sad music and wailing, the people followed their King to his last resting place in Dunfermline Abbey. . . .

Wrapped in a robe of cloth of gold the great King was laid to rest, and a beautiful tomb of white marble was raised over his grave. Long ago the tomb has disappeared, but the place where Robert the Bruce lies is still pointed out in the Abbey of Dunfermline.

True to his promise, the Douglas ordered the heart of Bruce to be taken from his body after he was dead. The heart was then embalmed. That is, it was prepared with sweet-smelling spices and other things to keep it from decay. Douglas enclosed the heart in a beautiful box of silver and enamel, which he hung round his neck by a chain of silk and gold. Then, with a noble company of knights and squires, he set sail for Palestine.

On his way he passed through Spain. There he heard that the King of Spain was fighting against the Saracens. The Saracens were the people who had possession of Palestine. They were unkind to the Christians, and insulted their religion. Douglas therefore thought that he would be doing right to help the King of Spain, before passing on to the Holy Land.

The armies met, and there was a great battle. The Scots charged so furiously that the Saracens fled before them. But thinking that the Spaniards were following to help them, the Scots chased the fleeing foe too far. Too late, Douglas found that he and his little band were cut off from their friends, and entirely surrounded by the fierce, dark faces of the enemy.

There was no escape. All that was left to do was to die fighting. Taking the silver box containing King Robert's heart from his neck, Douglas threw it into the thickest of the fight, crying, "On, gallant heart, as thou wert ever wont, the Douglas will follow thee or die." Then springing after it, he fiercely fought until he fell, pierced with many wounds. Round him fell most of the brave company of nobles who had set sail with him.

When the battle was over, the few who remained sought for their leader. They found him lying dead above the heart of Bruce.[1]

When we lay our life down for the heart of the King, we capture His passion and find our divine purpose. True greatness is only found as we die to selfish ambition, jealousy, envy and strife, and embrace a noble culture that manifests the heart of the King.

13

Iron Sharpens Iron

Nearly all men can stand adversity, but if you want to test a man's character, give him power.

Abraham Lincoln

If we are going to see famous people emerge from the Body of Christ, then it is imperative that we develop an empowering culture. But we must realize that empowering people means giving their latent tendencies, whether good, bad or ugly, opportunities to grow and find expression. And unless we have ways of confronting the bad and the ugly when they are exposed, we will make room for a kind of spiritual cancer in the Body.

Cancer cells are the fastest-growing cells in a body, but they live a self-absorbed existence, growing at the expense of everything else. They ultimately destroy the very thing that gave them life. Similarly, believers who allow selfish ambition to dictate their agendas instead of living to benefit the whole family become a cancer to the Body of Christ.

It is important to understand that certain cultural elements actually facilitate and encourage this sick social and spiritual dynamic. I experienced this firsthand many years ago when I was asked to help resolve a conflict between two leaders. One was a young man who had spent many years serving his senior leader in a vibrant church, with the promise of becoming the man's successor at a specified time. When that date came and went without any sign of the senior leader passing the baton, the younger leader began to get restless. After several conversations between them in which the senior leader felt as though he was being "pushed out," it became apparent that he had changed his mind and had decided not to step aside.

In time, the young associate pastor asked to be sent out to plant his own church. The senior leader agreed, threw a going-away party for him, took an offering for the new work and publicly encouraged his congregants to go with him. But a few months later, when the senior pastor found out that I was helping this younger brother start his church, he was livid. He called me and wanted to know what I was doing supporting a church split. When I recounted the facts as I understood them, he acknowledged that the story was accurate, but said that his former associate pastor (whom he had mentored for nearly two decades) was "an Absalom" (see 2 Samuel 13–15).

When I hung up the phone, I was confused. This senior leader had taken an offering for the younger leader, had publicly prayed for him and so on. Yet after the associate left, his mentor had decided he was an Absalom. I was supposed to talk to these leaders again the next day, so I decided to ask the Lord what I should do.

Immediately, the Lord said, *It takes a David to create an Absalom!*

I was stunned. David was a man after God's own heart (see Acts 13:22). *How could David help create an Absalom?* I inquired.

The Lord directed me to examine the books of Samuel in order to understand this unhealthy leadership dynamic. I want to share with you the insights I gained in that process.

Leading from Dysfunction

David was a dysfunctional leader after God's heart. Six of his many sons were born to him in Hebron from six different wives (see 2 Samuel 3:2–5). David's wife Ahinoam was mother to Amnon, who was David's oldest son. Amnon fell in love with Absalom's sister, Tamar, the daughter of Maacah, another of David's wives. When Amnon became aggressive in his pursuit of Tamar, she sent him packing. But he became so obsessed with her beauty that he violently raped her (see 2 Samuel 13:1–19). When word came to King David about his daughter's rape, he was incensed, but he did not do a darned thing about it, which turned out to be a pattern throughout his life. When Absalom found out about it, he took his violated sister into his home, where she stayed until the day she died.

Absalom's name means "my father is my peace." As his name suggests, he was a peacemaker, the kind of person who needs someone to bring justice to wrongs so there can be peace. As each day passed without any closure to the rape incident, Absalom's anger grew, until he secretly devised a plot to kill Amnon. After having Amnon murdered, Absalom fled the country to save his own life. He lived in exile for a number of years, yet longed for his father. Through a series of complex circumstances, he managed to get back into his dad's palace. But even though Amnon was dead, Absalom never forgave his father for not confronting him about Tamar's rape.

Bitterness escalated in Absalom until it possessed his soul. Revenge drove him to stand at the entrance of his father's courtroom for four years and tell people that they would get no justice in that court until he became king (see 2 Samuel 15:1–7). Eventually, Absalom convinced the Israelites that he was the righteous leader who would bring them justice. Ultimately, his self-promoting tactics won him the heart of the nation.

Can you imagine one of your kids undermining you for four years in your own house, with you never saying anything to him? Not even a little, "Hey, Ab, I heard you might have a . . . like . . . uh . . . slight disagreement with me over something." Yet that is exactly what David did. And it did not stop there; it got worse. Absalom finally gathered enough support to proclaim himself king of Israel. You would think his father finally would have confronted him at that point, right? *No!* Instead, David fled the country, going into exile and ordering his soldiers not to harm Absalom.

Meanwhile back at the throne, instead of giving the customary inauguration speech, Absalom pitched a tent on the roof of the palace and had sex with his father's concubines as all Israel watched (see 2 Samuel 16:22).

By now you might be asking yourself, *What the heck was that guy doing?* I will tell you what. By raping his father's women, he was taking revenge on his father for not rescuing Tamar from Amnon. He was sending a big, loud message to his dad: "How does it feel when someone violates the girls you care about and you are powerless to help them?" In other words, when injustice is unconfronted it gives birth to more injustice, ultimately creating legacies of bondage through mindsets of hopelessness.

The Things Giant Killers Fear

Absalom was not King David's only failure. David never confronted any of his sons, resulting in two of them usurping his throne and one raping his daughter. In fact, the king's dysfunction went far beyond the borders of his family. Joab, commander of David's armies and head of his mighty men, murdered one of Israel's best generals, yet he was allowed to retain his post and was never even court-martialed by the king (see 2 Samuel 3:27). When Solomon became king, David gave him a hit list of all the people he did not have the guts to confront when he was in power and ordered the young king to clean up his messes.

The private life of the man after God's heart reads like a disgusting soap opera. But the real question is, what caused a mighty man of God to kill giants, yet not confront his own men? Why would a man after God's heart—a man who had the courage to destroy with his bare hands wild animals that attacked his sheep, and who took on a nine-foot-six giant with a rock—not discipline his sons his entire life?

The answer lies in David's formative years as a young soldier serving an insane king. King Saul took David from a simple peasant family, moved him into his royal palace and raised him with his own son, Jonathan. But Saul became jealous of his adopted son and spent fourteen years trying to kill him. Like many leaders, David reacted to Saul's abusive authority in his life by going to the opposite extreme with his sons and soldiers. This created a culture in which people were empowered but were seldom confronted.

When Sons Become Enemies

After studying the life of David, I began to understand the unhealthy relational component that existed between my two pastor friends. Like David, many leaders hate confrontation. They know how to deal with enemies, but they have not learned the skill of disciplining their sons and daughters. This often results in leaders and/or fathers being passive, *until* their anger finally overcomes their fear of conflict.

When a leader has had enough, he usually changes the name of the violator to that of an adversary (Jezebel, Judas and Absalom are the most common choices). Then he brings his warrior weapons to a family affair, as Saul did when he hurled his spear at his son Jonathan at the dinner table, and at David before that. This never results in reconciliation, of course, because the goal of this kind of conflict is to destroy your enemy and protect your flock from wolves. When this kind of "confrontation" goes bad, it serves to validate the leader's misconception that talking to people about their "stuff" leads to the destruction of the relationship. This causes the leader to confront others even less, which results in injustice increasing all the more. Eventually, this cycle creates an environment as dysfunctional as that of King David's family.

As I investigated the relational dynamic between my two pastor friends, I discovered that this same Davidic pattern had existed between them from the inception of their friendship. The younger man had a strong personality, but he often lacked communication skills and boundaries. The older leader hated conflict. He was a peacekeeper (again, not to be confused with a peacemaker) and wanted harmony at all costs. But people can only stuff their feelings for so long before they begin to erode from the inside out. The senior leader eventually accumulated a case file so thick that it could no longer be contained in the file drawers of his heart.

When my friend was sent out to plant his own work, the geographic distance between the two of them created a sense of safety for the senior leader. He finally felt he could articulate his feelings of being dishonored, afraid, controlled and run over for almost two decades. But the associate leader had no idea of how he had been affecting his previous environment, because he had seldom received feedback that was not articulated in anger. When his senior leader was angry with him, he would defend himself from his leader's advice instead of assimilating it. Consequently, he grew very little in the areas that were irritations to his mentor. The senior pastor finally concluded that this young man was an enemy, since only enemies tried to hurt people. In his mind, the Absalom title therefore seemed to fit the young man perfectly.

Passive Jesus?

Christian leaders tend to spiritualize their dysfunctions by using Scripture that is contextually irrelevant to the core problems of their hearts. People who fear confrontation, for instance, often cite Bible verses about turning the other cheek or loving our enemies (see Matthew 5:39, 44). But we are not talking about enemies here. We are talking about family, friends and team members. And we cannot afford to ignore the many Scriptures about living a life of confrontation. For example, Proverbs says, "Faithful are the wounds of a friend, but deceitful are the kisses of an enemy," and "Iron sharpens iron, so one man sharpens another" (Proverbs 27:6, 17).

Some people think Jesus was passive, but nothing could be further from the truth. His words and actions were the most confrontational in the Bible. Let's look at the way Jesus dealt with a few different groups of people. Here is His response to His disciples, who did not seem to have the faith to cast a demon out of a kid:

> One of the crowd answered Him, "Teacher, I brought You my son, possessed with a spirit which makes him mute; and whenever it seizes him, it slams him to the ground and he foams at the mouth, and grinds his teeth and stiffens out. I told Your disciples to cast it out, and they could not do it." And He answered them

and said, "O unbelieving generation, how long shall I be with you? How long shall I put up with you? Bring him to Me!"

Mark 9:17–19

Or check out this one. Jesus took exception to some business people selling their stuff at the Temple, so He made a whip and drove them out. (Do you think He actually hit anyone? Yikes!)

The Passover of the Jews was near, and Jesus went up to Jerusalem. And He found in the temple those who were selling oxen and sheep and doves, and the money changers seated at their tables. And He made a scourge of cords, and drove them all out of the temple, with the sheep and the oxen; and He poured out the coins of the money changers and overturned their tables; and to those who were selling the doves He said, "Take these things away; stop making My Father's house a place of business."

John 2:13–16

But Jesus' favorite targets of confrontation were the religious leaders of His day. He did not have much patience for their self-righteous, ego-centered ministry style:

Woe to you, scribes and Pharisees, hypocrites! For you clean the outside of the cup and of the dish, but inside they are full of robbery and self-indulgence. You blind Pharisee, first clean the inside of the cup and of the dish, so that the outside of it may become clean also.

Woe to you, scribes and Pharisees, hypocrites! For you are like whitewashed tombs, which on the outside appear beautiful, but inside they are full of dead men's bones and all uncleanness. So you, too, outwardly appear righteous to men, but inwardly you are full of hypocrisy and lawlessness.

Matthew 23:25–28

I would like to suggest that Jesus had no problem speaking His mind to people. You always knew where you stood with Him.

The Art of Confrontation

Of course, when Jesus walked the earth, He had a few advantages over us. Minor things like the fact that He never sinned, for instance, so He never had to worry about hypocritically pointing out faults in others while neglecting His own. He was also God and knew the hearts of men, so His assessment of people's motives was always accurate. Undoubtedly, these advantages gave Him confidence and grace when it came to approaching confrontation; He was neither shy nor overly harsh.

We, on the other hand, have to be told, "Brethren, even if anyone is caught in any trespass, you who are spiritual, restore such a one in a spirit of gentleness; each one looking to yourself, so that you too will not be tempted" (Galatians 6:1). According to this standard, confrontation must never involve yelling at someone, accusing him or her of evil, venting frustration or punishing the person for failing at something or hurting you. We must be especially careful about not judging people's motives. In my experience, our so-called "gift of discernment" often turns out to be *suspicion* in disguise, especially when we are upset with someone.

Over the years, I have learned these seven principles for practicing the art of healthy confrontation:

1. When a problem arises, make an appointment to talk to the person as soon as possible. Waiting too long allows the seed of bitterness to gestate. Don't wait for anger to be your counselor. Remember, this is not about punishing the person for inappropriate behavior. You are meeting for his or her benefit. The goal is to help mold the person into the image of God and reconcile your relationship.

2. Let the person know how his or her behavior has affected you. Describe in detail how the actions in question are making you *feel*.

Keep your armor off by being transparent about your own struggles. When a person is responding to you, *listen from your heart to his or her heart*. Many people are not good at articulating their struggles, so you often have to listen beyond their words. As the person is speaking to you, don't develop your defenses or turn the conversation into a war of words. Ask questions that unearth the root problem. What is really wrong? What kind of core problem would cause these symptoms? Always give the person the benefit of the doubt, no matter how he or she has behaved. Remind yourself that the person you are having a problem with was made in the image of God and therefore most likely has a good heart, even though his or her behavior is negatively affecting the environment. Never think of the person as an enemy, but instead as a wayward son or daughter (or a father or mother). Show honor at all times. Let the person know you believe in him or her. Remember, you only have as much influence in someone's life as that person has value for you.

3. Ask the person how you can be part of the solution. By this time, you may have found out that you are actually part of the problem. Maybe you are King David in this situation. Has your fear, weakness or dysfunction become a seedbed for that person's strength to be overemphasized or for his or her weakness to be exposed? Have you reacted to the way you were raised or to some negative circumstances in your own life?

4. If other people are not part of the problem or part of the solution, it is none of their business. Don't talk to other people about your offense. Don't build a case against the person by bringing up other people's names in the conversation or saying things like, "I talked to John and Mary, and they have the same problem with you." This just makes

you look like a coward and a gossip. If you do that, don't be surprised if the person being confronted feels like he or she is a victim of a gang assault. You are not there to be someone's prosecuting attorney.

On this note, if someone comes to you to talk about a problem with someone else, tell him or her to go talk directly to the person, not to you. I have 550 employees who work for me at Bethel Church. Many of my team members used to come up to me and begin telling me about a struggle they were having with another staff member. Before they got twenty seconds into their discourse, I would interrupt them and ask, "Have you talked to this person yet?" Nine times out of ten they would say no. Then I would ask them, "What business do you have talking to me if you haven't even talked to the person who offended you?"

It is important to remember that a person who talks to you about someone else will one day be talking to someone else about you. Allowing people to complain about others creates a culture of gossip. Personally, I will not tolerate it at Bethel.

5. If you realize during the conversation that you are the problem or part of the dilemma, be quick to repent. Humility always leads to repentance. Don't defend yourself; leave your weapons outside the door. If the other person is wrong, verbally forgive him or her. Forgiveness restores the standard, so once there is repentance treat the person as if he or she never sinned.

6. If you come to an impasse, have someone you *both* respect equally join you in another meeting to help resolve the issue. Bringing someone whom one of the parties does not respect into the meeting will only make it feel as if the other person's attorney is present. But a wise person

who is not emotionally attached to the conflict can bring insightful perspective that is hard for either party to see in the middle of a conflict. That outside perspective will usually help bring the necessary resolution. I cannot count the number of times I have had a problem with someone, only to find out in a meeting with him or her that I was the problem. Having a respected third party present helped me see the truth.

7. Last but not least, don't withdraw from the person after a conflict. Make an extra effort to stay close to him or her during the healing process. This is often the difference between a long, healthy relationship and a lifelong pattern of conflict.

Many years ago, a study was done in the business world concerning the issue of conflict. The study showed that when a customer had a problem with a business and the company satisfactorily resolved the issue, the customer became many times more loyal to the store in the years that followed than he or she was before the conflict. Likewise, I believe that conflict and confrontation resolved inside the core values of the Kingdom actually strengthen our relationships. These struggles are the sign of real relationships where people feel safe to tell one another the truth in love. This creates covenant societies that bond around family values, instead of fatherless sibling rivalries where orphans vie for preeminence in the pecking order of the world's chicken coop.

It Takes All Kinds

It takes all kinds of people to make the world go round. My mother often said that to me when I was growing up. The older I get, the more I realize she was right. There are black-and-white thinkers like Absalom, who view the world through the lens of justice. They see life as a long journey down the path of wrong and right, good and evil. If people wired like this witness an injustice or are mistreated somehow, they often become obsessed with the need for closure. If they live in an environment where conflict is looked down on or is not allowed, they tend to come apart inside.

There is an entirely different type of person who views the world in shades of gray. Some of these people just don't like conflict, but others just don't see the need for it. These are the mercy givers of the world who walk in extreme grace. They are not easily offended, and they have a high capacity for forgiveness without the need for much articulation. They just naturally trust people, giving others the benefit of the doubt in most situations.

Trouble can arise when you yoke these two extremely different types of people together. I counseled a pastor and his family some years ago where this dynamic had nearly destroyed their family. The pastor was fired from his senior position over some false rumors going around in the church he had planted. He refused to defend himself or his family, believing that the truth would eventually speak for itself.

But this pastor's seventeen-year-old son was a justice guy. He needed his dad to step up to the plate and defend the family. When his father refused, he grew angry with him and began to hate the congregation and the Church in general. This young man, who had once been an on-fire leader of his youth group, became a furious, resentful son.

When I counseled with them, I could see the root of the problem within a few minutes. Mr. Grace was yoked to Mr. Justice in a major conflict, and they each had different needs in order to reach a resolution. The dilemma was finally resolved when I suggested that the family have a meeting with the board that had fired the pastor. In the meeting, the young man was empowered to share how the leadership's decisions had affected him and how unfairly he felt the family was treated. The family went on to pastor another church, and the son became their youth pastor. Sometimes sharing what is on your heart releases you from the need to be right.

Mr. Grace Meets Mr. Justice

Bill Johnson and I have worked together for more than three decades. He is Mr. Grace, and I am Mr. Justice. When we have a conflict with someone in our movement, Bill is almost always at the spearhead of mercy. He is quick to forgive and restore people to their calling. He believes the best about everyone and rarely says a negative word about anyone.

As Mr. Justice, I am pretty quick to forgive, but much slower to trust someone again. Bill tends to trust people until they prove they are untrustworthy. I tend not to trust people until they have earned it.

This difference in perspective has caused some interesting challenges throughout our lives. But the key to our success has been in valuing each other's opinions and listening to one another's perspectives. It is important to remember that just because someone approaches a problem differently than you would does not make that person wrong. I owe much of my personal success to Bill's gift of mercy. Whenever I have a conflict with Bill's paradigm, I remind myself that it is his mindset that has been the catalyst for my ministry. Bill believed in me before I deserved it! May mercy and truth kiss in the palace of hope.

14

::

Casting Vision
and Capturing Hearts

If you look at the past long enough, you will become a
monument instead of a movement.

Bill Johnson

On December 15, 1966, Walt Disney died, and the world lost
one of its greatest Imagineers (Walt's word for dreamers
and visionaries). But five years after his death, his greatest
dream of all was actualized. Walt Disney had envisioned a theme
park so awesome that it created a fantasy world where families could leave the troubles of the outside world behind them.
On October 1, 1971, Walt Disney World officially opened in
Orlando, Florida. Walt's brother, Roy, presided over the ribbon-
cutting ceremony.

In the midst of the celebration, somebody came up to Roy and said, "It's too bad Walt couldn't be here to see this."

Roy responded, "He did see this, and that's why you can see it today."

The author of Hebrews agrees with Roy when it proclaims, "What is seen was not made out of things which are visible" (Hebrews 11:3). This verse speaks of how God creates. He was the original Imagineer, and what He *envisioned* we became.

We can also create visible realities from the invisible dimension of our imaginations. In fact, there has never been anything perceived in the visible world that was not first assembled in the invisible realm of the imagination. Jacob's experience with spotted and speckled sheep, recorded in Genesis 30, illustrates this principle. Jacob worked for his father-in-law, Laban, for a long time. After twenty turbulent years of mistrust and dishonesty, Jacob was ready to leave. He told his father-in-law to give him what was his so he could go his own way. Although Laban was a liar and a cheat, he was no fool. He knew that Jacob was making him a fortune. Laban told Jacob to name his wages and stay.

Jacob knew that no matter what his wages were, his father-in-law would find some way to swindle him out of them. He had to come up with a foolproof plan so Laban could not take advantage of him. Finally, he got this crazy idea. He told Laban that he would work for all the spotted and speckled sheep and goats. They struck a deal, and then the story takes on a bizarre twist. Jacob carved spots and speckles in some branches and put them in front of the watering hole whenever the strongest sheep and goats were mating there. What happened next is pretty amazing. Those sheep and goats began giving birth to spotted and speckled offspring.

As I pondered this strange passage, it dawned on me that this is not a lesson in agriculture. It is a parable of how we,

His sheep, reproduce through our imagination. The watering hole is a place of *reflection*. It represents the place where we imagine, dream and envision the future with God. As we meditate on these things, our hearts become "wombs" in which we gestate our ideas like seeds until we give birth to them as offspring.

As human beings, we reach our highest potential when we harness the power of our imagination to birth the realities and purposes of God for us and for the world. When we dream with God, as Mary did, *we* co-create masterpieces of *His* imagination. Bill Johnson captures this supernatural reality well in his book *Secrets to Imitating God* (Destiny Image, 2009).

Vision Gives Pain a Purpose

I am not saying that if you imagine a pink elephant, you are going to give birth to it. I am simply trying to demonstrate the supernatural principle of envisioning. The New Age movement has been teaching this for years, which has led many Christian leaders to think that the idea is from hell. But the truth is that New Age leaders are stealing our stuff, and by reacting to them, we have lost the creative power of visualizing.

Let me be a little more pragmatic for a moment. This supernatural principle basically works like this: When we imagine something in our mind's eye, a phenomenon occurs in our spirit that causes us to want to see with our natural eyes what we have perceived in our heart.

Michelangelo put it like this: "I saw the angel in the marble and carved until I set him free." He looked at a boulder with his natural eyes, and with his imagination he pictured an angel imprisoned in the stone. This motivated him to chip away at the rock relentlessly until he could view on the outside what he imagined on the inside. When people envision something—especially something from God—it creates a naturally supernatural impetus to apprehend the vision and see it fulfilled, built, funded and otherwise realized.

Solomon said, "Where there is no vision, the people are unrestrained [wander aimlessly], but happy is he who keeps the law" (Proverbs 29:18). The King James Version says it this way: "Where there is no vision, the people perish: but he that keepeth the law, happy is he." When people lack vision, they lead unrestrained lives. Their life's motivation is reduced to staying out of pain or finding pleasure. This may seem like Easy Street, but it is actually the path to a mundane, boring existence that ultimately undermines God's divine destiny in people's lives.

As blind Helen Keller said, "It is a terrible thing to see and have no vision." But when people catch a vision, they will "keep the law." In other words, they will restrain their options to apprehend their vision. Vision not only gives us focused energy that empowers us to say no to certain things and yes to others; it also gives us the courage to endure difficulties in the path to our destiny.

Let me illustrate. An overweight person goes to the gym to get in shape. But the morning after his first workout, he is so sore that he can hardly get out of bed. If he has a vision (if he can picture himself with a great body), that vision will give his pain a purpose. It is vision that causes him to restrain his eating, reorder his schedule and push past the discomfort of muscle pain to obtain his goal. On the other hand, it is difficult to get skinny by hating being fat, because reacting to a negative rarely creates a positive.

Vision is the invisible manager that guides, encourages and inspires fervent souls who are undertaking the Master's supernatural assignment to prepare the planet for His reentry. When I see saints exercising enormous self-control, showing great courage in overcoming difficulties and demonstrating excellence in their divine assignments, I know it means they have captured a vision for their lives.

I am reminded of the old fable of the three bricklayers all working on the same long wall. Someone came up to the first man laying bricks and asked, "Sir, may I ask what you are doing?"

"I'm laying bricks," he snapped sarcastically. "What does it look like I'm doing?"

The man approached the second bricklayer and asked, "What are you doing?"

"I'm building a wall. That's what I'm doing."

Finally, the inquisitive onlooker approached the last mason, finding him hard at work laying bricks with exceptional excellence and speed. "Mister, could I trouble you with a question? What is it you're doing?" the man asked in admiration.

Still hard at work, the bricklayer answered, "I'm building a great cathedral for God."

Which mason would you want working for you?

Vision-Based Discipline

In September 1998, we founded the Bethel School of Supernatural Ministry with 37 students. Over the past 18 years, the school has grown to more than 2,100 full-time students. One of the greatest challenges we have faced over the years is getting the students to discipline themselves to come to class on time, do their work, pay their tuition and so on, without creating a controlling environment. In the early years of our school, I spent many hours with my staff deliberating over different methods of motivating the students. What we realized over time was that most of these ideas were really just systematic levels of punishment dished out to those violating our laws.

Finally, we stumbled upon Solomon's words and realized that it is vision that causes people to keep the law. When people lose their vision, they no longer keep the rules, restrain their options or live disciplined lives. This revelation changed our entire leadership approach. Now when students act inappropriately, we simply ask them what their vision looks like for their lives. Rarely can they articulate it, because somewhere between the time they decided to make the huge sacrifice required to attend our school and the time they started misbehaving, they lost their vision. Their screen went blank, their hard drive crashed and they stopped dreaming.

Our primary goal at that point becomes helping them rediscover, redeem and reenvision their lives. Often, we accomplish this simply by having them recount the story of their journey to the school. We ask them questions like, "What inspired you to come to this supernatural school in the first place?" "What were you hoping would happen to you when you came here?" "Share with us in picture form what you thought it was going to look like when you graduated from BSSM."

Frequently, there are tears as such students recount the vision that motivated them to take the plunge. Sometimes the treasure of their vision is buried so deep in the soil of disappointment, discouragement or disillusionment that they need help unearthing it. This is where the gifts of the Spirit come in handy. In these situations, we often will ask the Holy Spirit to give us a prophetic word that restores the student's vision and encourages him or her to press past the pain to obtain the prize.

I should make it clear that we do believe in discipline at BSSM (see Hebrews 12:7–13). We understand very well that vision is not the magical answer to everyone's problem. It is, however, a powerful principle in the hands of the Master Potter.

Imparting Mission and Vision

If we are going to transform cities and make disciples of all nations, we need to capture God's vision for them. One of the struggles I have often encountered in this area is people's confusion between *having a mission* and *catching a vision*. I have often heard leaders use the words *mission* and *vision* interchangeably, as if they are the same thing. But they are not the same thing. Mission is the *why*—the reason or purpose and heart motivation behind what we are trying to accomplish. Vision means *what* the mission looks like. It is not really a vision unless you can *see it*. You can do a great job of articulating a mission, but unless people can *see it* in their mind's eye, they remain restrained in their ability to help build it.

For example, I can tell you all the reasons why we need an orphanage in Kenya, Africa. I can explain to you the extreme negative social conditions that AIDS has created in that country. I can describe to you in detail the destructive nature of poverty that looms heavily over that nation. You may even fly there to help construct the facility. But you cannot build a successful structure without seeing the blueprints.

A leader's ability to envision a mission and then impart it to others is what separates good leaders from great leaders. Great leaders have the unique ability to picture the purposes of God in their spirit and then impart the picture to others. You know that people have captured the vision not when they can repeat it (a parrot can do that), but when they can see it in their spirit. It is *vision* that impregnates people with the need to labor to give birth to a *mission*.

Many times I have watched as leaders passionately communicate a mission to people, carefully and meticulously explaining every detail of the purposes behind their plan. But then they give their audience no idea, no vision, of what it actually looks like. Sometimes a mission will capture people's hearts and cause them to give to a project for a season. But sustained, disciplined help usually comes from people who can envision what the mission looks like, because vision motivates them from the inside.

Repeating the mission, making fervent pleas or causing people to feel guilty for not making a contribution or a sacrifice is not the way to impart vision. Although these methods may bear some fruit at times, they most often are related to manipulation, which is rooted in witchcraft. Such external motivators never bring out excellence, passion and initiative in people.

The greater the mission is, the clearer the vision must be, because huge assignments usually require high levels of sacrifice and/or risk in seeing them fulfilled. The level of sacrifice a mission requires determines the measure of clarity necessary for people to follow through. When a leader lacks the skill to impart vision, sacrifice begins to separate the people who can instinctively envision from those who cannot.

It is for this reason that real estate developers will spend thousands of dollars constructing models of their building ventures to help bankers and financiers catch the vision for their projects. Though this adds to the cost of the development, experienced developers realize that investors are not always the greatest visionaries and must be inspired externally. They know that if they can somehow get the financial backers to *see* the project, such potential investors are much more likely to take a risk and fund it.

Leaders need to invest their resources in inspiring faith in their people. It takes faith to capture a grand mission and vision. Without a mission from God, the greatest visions in life are no more than the worthless efforts of self-righteous souls who climb the high mountains of human significance, only to see their passion perish in the thin air of human applause.

But without vision, God's holy intentions lay buried deep in our souls. His words never become flesh and His righteous purposes remain imprisoned in the small minds of those who refuse to dream with their Creator. Instead, they bury their talents in the hard soil of comfort and complacency. It is mission that inspires passion and zeal, while vision provokes perseverance and sacrifice.

Seizing the Promised Land

There is another element of vision that leaders must successfully clarify in order to inspire their people to sacrifice for the mission. We see this element in the story of Moses trying to lead the Israelites into the Promised Land. Moses had to figure out a way to inspire former slaves to capture a vision for a better life on the other side of the river. But the nature of slavery is such that you never really learn to dream. The slave nature produces controlling cultures, and such cultures resist thinking and thus create *dream-free zones.*

Moses' strategy to awaken the Israelites' imaginations was similar to the real estate developers' strategy. He knew the best way to impart vision to these slaves was to arouse their five senses with the fruit of their promises. So he sent spies into the Promised Land and commanded them to come back with a detailed report about the land's topography, inhabitants, infrastructure and produce. He also instructed them to make every effort to bring back some fruit from the land:

> When Moses sent them to spy out the land of Canaan, he said to them, "Go up there into the Negev; then go up into the hill country. See what the land is like, and whether the people who live in it are strong or weak, whether they are few or many. How is the land in which they live, is it good or bad? And how are the cities in which they live, are they like

open camps or with fortifications? How is the land, is it fat or lean? Are there trees in it or not? Make an effort then to get some of the fruit of the land." Now the time was the time of the first ripe grapes.

So they went up and spied out the land from the wilderness of Zin as far as Rehob, at Lebo-hamath. When they had gone up into the Negev, they came to Hebron where Ahiman, Sheshai and Talmai, the descendants of Anak were. (Now Hebron was built seven years before Zoan in Egypt.)

Then they came to the valley of Eshcol and from there cut down a branch with a single cluster of grapes; and they carried it on a pole between two men, with some of the pomegranates and the figs. That place was called the valley of Eshcol, because of the cluster, which the sons of Israel cut down from there.

When they returned from spying out the land, at the end of forty days, they proceeded to come to Moses and Aaron and to all the congregation of the sons of Israel in the wilderness of Paran, at Kadesh; and they brought back word to them and to all the congregation and showed them the fruit of the land. Thus they told him, and said, "We went in to the land where you sent us; and it certainly does flow with milk and honey, and this is its fruit."

Numbers 13:17–27

When the spies returned, gave their report and displayed the fruit they had brought back, the Israelites heard, saw, felt, smelled and tasted the vision of the Promised Land. Moses did his best to stimulate their five senses so that they could imagine the land and give birth to a nation. But ten of the twelve spies Moses sent let their fears dictate their worldview, and they sabotaged the purposes of God in the hearts of the people. Here is the account:

Caleb quieted the people before Moses and said, "We should by all means go up and take possession of it, for we will surely overcome it." But the men who had gone up with him said, "We

are not able to go up against the people; for they are too strong
for us." So they gave out to the sons of Israel a bad report of
the land which they had spied out, saying, "The land through
which we have gone, in spying it out, is a land that devours its
inhabitants; and all the people whom we saw in it are men of
great size. There also we saw the Nephilim (the sons of Anak
are part of the Nephilim); and we became like grasshoppers in
our own sight, and so we were in their sight."

Numbers 13:30–33

Entrenched in their slave mentality, the people believed these
ten spies' bad report and started talking about going back to
Egypt. P. K. Bernard was right when he said, "A man without a
vision is a man without a future. A man without a future will
always return to his past." People who insist on living in the
"good old days" cannot "in-vision." They just don't understand
that when your memories are greater than your dreams, you
are already dying.

Most of the Israelites never did get it. They wandered aim-
lessly in the wilderness, and many of them perished. Their
inability to capture the vision was rooted in their failure to
embrace their identity as God's covenant people. They forgot
the miracles of God in the wilderness and envisioned themselves as grasshoppers in the Promised Land. Low self-esteem
will always make you feel like a bug in a land full of giants just
waiting to squash your dreams.

Unlike the rest of the Israelites, Joshua and Caleb embraced
their God-given identity, which allowed God's vision to be etched
deeply within their hearts. They alone came back and gave a
good report. More than forty years passed before their dream
was realized, yet their hearts still burned for the Promised Land.
Caleb was one of the chief Imagineers of Israel. Here is his
exhortation to Joshua when they finally entered the land of
promise as old men:

Then the sons of Judah drew near to Joshua in Gilgal, and Caleb the son of Jephunneh the Kenizzite said to him, "You know the word which the LORD spoke to Moses the man of God concerning you and me in Kadesh-barnea. I was forty years old when Moses the servant of the LORD sent me from Kadesh-barnea to spy out the land, and I brought word back to him as it was in my heart. Nevertheless my brethren who went up with me made the heart of the people melt with fear; but I followed the LORD my God fully. So Moses swore on that day, saying, 'Surely the land on which your foot has trodden will be an inheritance to you and to your children forever, because you have followed the LORD my God fully.' Now behold, the LORD has let me live, just as He spoke, these forty-five years, from the time that the LORD spoke this word to Moses, when Israel walked in the wilderness; and now behold, I am eighty-five years old today. I am still as strong today as I was in the day Moses sent me; as my strength was then, so my strength is now, for war and for going out and coming in. Now then, give me this hill country about which the LORD spoke on that day, for you heard on that day that Anakim were there, with great fortified cities; perhaps the LORD will be with me, and I will drive them out as the LORD has spoken."

So Joshua blessed him and gave Hebron to Caleb the son of Jephunneh for an inheritance.

Joshua 14:6–13

The question is, are you a grasshopper lost in the thorn-infested fields of life, or are you a child of the King, called to destroy the works of the devil?

Inspiring a Movement

Movements are always birthed by dreamers who first envision life as it ought to be and not as it is. Dreamers stir people's imaginations, agitate their souls and inspire their hearts. George

Bernard Shaw expressed the dreamer's attitude when he said, "Some men see things as they are and ask 'Why?' Others dream of things that never were and ask, 'Why not?'"

Dreamers are the cultural catalysts, reformers and history makers. In order for us to experience the fulfillment of the Lord's Prayer, "Your kingdom come. Your will be done, on earth as it is in heaven" (Matthew 6:10), it is vital that we begin to envision the world not as it is, but as it ought to be.

Dr. Martin Luther King Jr. is one of the best examples of someone who saw the world the way God intended it to be and altered the course of American history. On August 28, 1963, Dr. King imparted a vision for the equality of all races to an entire generation of people. Although he proclaimed this vision decades ago, it still echoes through the halls of our history. Here is a portion of his speech titled "I Have a Dream":

I have a dream that one day this nation will rise up and live out the true meaning of its creed: "We hold these truths to be self-evident, that all men are created equal."

I have a dream that one day on the red hills of Georgia, the sons of former slaves and the sons of former slave owners will be able to sit down together at the table of brotherhood.

I have a dream that one day even the state of Mississippi, a state sweltering with the heat of injustice, sweltering with the heat of oppression, will be transformed into an oasis of freedom and justice.

I have a dream that my four little children will one day live in a nation where they will not be judged by the color of their skin but by the content of their character. . . .

I have a dream that one day, down in Alabama, with its vicious racists, with its governor having his lips dripping with the words of "interposition" and "nullification"—one day right there in Alabama little black boys and black girls will be able to join hands with little white boys and white girls as sisters and brothers. . . .

I have a dream that one day every valley shall be exalted, and every hill and mountain shall be made low, the rough places will be made plain, and the crooked places will be made straight; "and the glory of the Lord shall be revealed and all flesh shall see it together."[1]

It is important to note *how* Dr. King, one of the greatest revolutionaries ever to grace this planet, inspired people to sacrifice for the cause. Like an artist, he used words to paint extraordinary portraits of freedom on the canvas of our imaginations. Every sentence was another stroke of the master's brush, impregnating the minds of his listeners to labor for liberty and struggle for freedom. Dr. King imparted his vision of heaven on earth until the day he died. On April 3, 1968, in Memphis, Tennessee, the day before he was assassinated, he gave his final public address, titled "I've Been to the Mountaintop." Here is an excerpt:

> I left Atlanta this morning, and as we got started on the plane, there were six of us. The pilot said over the public address system, "We are sorry for the delay, but we have Dr. Martin Luther King on the plane. And to be sure that all of the bags were checked, and to be sure that nothing would be wrong with the plane, we had to check out everything carefully. And we've had the plane protected and guarded all night."
>
> And then I got to Memphis. And some began to say the threats, or talk about the threats that were out. What would happen to me from some of our sick white brothers?
>
> Well, I don't know what will happen now. We've got some difficult days ahead. But it doesn't matter with me now. *Because I've been to the mountaintop.* And I don't mind. Like anybody, I would like to live a long life. Longevity has its place. But I'm not concerned about that now. I just want to do God's will. *And He's allowed me to go up to the mountain. And I've looked over. And I've seen the Promised Land.* I may not get there with you. But I want you to know tonight, that we, as a people, will get to the Promised Land. And I'm happy, tonight. I'm not worried about anything. I'm not fearing any man. Mine eyes have seen the glory of the coming of the Lord.[2]

The Downpour of the Spirit

We need a new generation of people who have the courage of Dr. King to once again rise out of the valley of despair and climb the mountain of revelation. This journey is not for a few chosen people but for a royal race of noblemen. May I remind you of the promise of the day in which we live, a day that began two millennia ago when the apostle Peter quoted the prophet Joel in the book of Acts:

> "It shall be in the last days," God says, "that I will pour forth of My Spirit on all mankind; and your sons and your daughters shall prophesy, and your young men shall see visions, and your old men shall dream dreams; even on My bondslaves, both men and women, I will in those days pour forth of My Spirit and they shall prophesy. And I will grant wonders in the sky above and signs on the earth below, blood, and fire, and vapor of smoke. The sun will be turned into darkness and the moon into blood, before the great and glorious day of the Lord shall come. And it shall be that everyone who calls on the name of the LORD will be saved."
>
> Acts 2:17–21

In these last days, God promises to pour out His Spirit on *everyone*. One of the main manifestations of this *heavy rain* is that old folks begin to dream again, while God infuses young people with His visions. Supernatural vision and God-inspired dreams are freely available to all who will seek this outpouring. And with more than four billion lost people on this planet, there has never been a more urgent need for Kingdom Imagineers, royal people and radical visionaries who sit in heavenly places with Christ and dream with God. It is time that we stop complaining about our circumstances and journey to the top of the mountain. It is from these heights that we will envision the world not as it is, but as God intended it to be.

I want to ask you again, what would your city look like if the Kingdom of God were superimposed over every realm of society? Can you imagine what would happen to the crime rate, the divorce rate, terminal diseases, hate, abortion, depression, poverty, hopelessness, molestation, rape, pornography, addictions, unemployment . . . if you and other dreamers began to envision the future of your city with God and then impregnated the populace with that vision, as Dr. Martin Luther King Jr. did in his day?

Dreamers and visionaries, take your places in the downpour of the Spirit's rain. Let it fill the pores of your soul with hope that feels, faith that sees and love that never fails!

15

:::

Impregnating the Cosmos

Prophecy is history written in advance.

Graham Cooke

The year is 907 BC, and the Israelites' king has managed to lead them away from God, into idolatry. His name is Jeroboam. He begins his reign by setting up two golden calves and demanding that his people worship them instead of worshiping Jehovah.

In the midst of the king's insanity, an unnamed prophet steps onto the scene and somehow manages to get into the king's presence. The prophet rebukes Jeroboam and declares that another king named Josiah is coming to restore Israel back to God. He prophesies to the wicked altar Jeroboam has built, saying that Josiah will sacrifice its evil priests upon it: "Behold, a son shall be born to the house of David, Josiah by name; and on you he shall sacrifice the priests of the high places who burn incense on you, and human bones shall be burned on you" (1 Kings 13:2). Then this prophet puts an exclamation point on his declaration: "This is the sign which the Lord has spoken, 'Behold, the altar shall be split apart and the ashes which are on it shall be poured out'" (verse 3).

As King Jeroboam stretches out his hand and yells to his guards to seize the prophet, his arm becomes paralyzed and hangs useless by his side. The prophet calls for God to heal the king, and God restores him. The man of God exits the place a little heated as the altar splits in half and the ashes pour out (see the full story in 1 Kings 12–13).

Two hundred and seventy years pass, and things continue to decline in Judah. King Manasseh's 55-year reign of terror plunges the country into one of the darkest seasons in its history. Thousands of children are sacrificed on the altars of idols, and the streets of Israel are filled with blood. It seems that no end to the bloodshed is in sight when Manasseh's son Amon takes the throne after his father's death and continues carrying out his father's evil agenda. But two years into Amon's reign, he is assassinated (see 2 Kings 21:19–24).

This is where the plot thickens. It is now 640 BC, and Josiah is crowned king at 8 years of age. When he turns 26, for some seemingly unknown reason he begins to seek the Lord, breaking generational curses passed down to him by his father and grandfather. Josiah calls for the restoration of the house of the LORD, which has not been used in more than half a century.

In the middle of the renovation project, Hilkiah, the high priest, finds a lost book of the Law hidden in the Temple someplace, one of the only copies to survive Manasseh's reign of terror. Hilkiah gives the book to Shaphan the scribe, who rushes into the king's chambers and reads it to Josiah. His reaction is swift and intense: "When the king heard the words of the book of the law, he tore his clothes" (2 Kings 22:11). From that point on, Josiah becomes a radical revivalist. He tears down the altars of Baal, destroys the evil priesthood, burns everything dedicated to the worship of other gods and calls the nation back to Jehovah.

But what really happens on that fateful day when, for the first time in his life, Josiah hears the Word of God? Some things are clear. The king realizes how far Judah has fallen from God's standard and how badly its people deserve to be judged. But something else happens. Josiah not only hears the Word of God for Judah; he also receives a prophetic word for himself. He embraces the declaration and seizes his destiny—all because a prophet has looked into the future and has called something that was not as though it were:

> Furthermore, the altar that was at Bethel and the high place which Jeroboam the son of Nebat, who made Israel sin, had made, even that altar and the high place he broke down. Then he demolished its stones, ground them to dust, and burned the Asherah. Now when Josiah turned, he saw the graves that were there on the mountain, and he sent and took the bones from the graves and burned them on the altar and defiled it according to the word of the LORD which the man of God proclaimed, who proclaimed these things.
>
> 2 Kings 23:15–16

Imagine what it must have been like for Josiah to realize that a prophet had called him by name and had declared his destiny hundreds of years before he was born. When he heard the word, Josiah understood that he had a God-given destiny, that his life was not an accident or just the fruit of an intimate moment between his parents. No, he had a race to run, a purpose to fulfill and a mark to make for God. He had been alive somewhere in the heart of God years before he had come forth into this world, and now it was his appointed time to challenge an ungodly system and make history (see 2 Kings 22–23).

Words Become Worlds

Now let's fast-forward about another seven hundred years. Peter and John are right outside the gate called Beautiful that leads to the Temple. A man lame from birth is sitting at the entrance of the gate. He is begging for money, but the apostles are broke. So Peter grabs the guy, pulls him to his feet and commands him to walk. You know the rest of the story—the lame man is completely healed and starts going nuts. A bunch of people gather around, trying to figure out what all the commotion is about. Peter takes the opportunity to preach to the crowd. At the end of his message he makes this statement:

> All the prophets who have spoken, from Samuel and his successors onward, also announced these days. It is you who are the sons of the prophets and of the covenant which God made with your fathers, saying to Abraham, "And in your seed all the families of the earth shall be blessed."
>
> Acts 3:24–25

What did Peter mean, "It is you who are the sons of the prophets"? He was teaching us how history becomes *His*-story. He was saying that the prophet Samuel and all the prophets after him looked into the future and saw a race of people who had never graced this planet before. As they perceived these people, they began to prophesy about them. Their prophecies impregnated the "womb of the dawn" (Psalm 110:3), if you will, with the "sperm" of God Himself. A completely new species of being was born from their prophetic declarations. Just as in the days of Jeroboam, when the unnamed prophet spoke of a king named Josiah, Samuel and his successors also saw us and called us into being.

Let me see if I can make this principle a little clearer. Jesus told a parable about a sower who planted seed in different types of soil. He said that the seed was the Word of God and the soil was our hearts in varying conditions (see Matthew 13:3–23). The Greek word *seed* in this text is the word *sperma*, from which we get the English word *sperm*. When the Word of the Lord is released into our hearts, we become impregnated with the Father's DNA and give birth to His nature in our lives.

Paul referred to this when he wrote, "My children, with whom I am again in labor until Christ is formed in you" (Galatians 4:19). How did Paul labor among them? He preached the Word of God, and as he spoke they were impregnated with the seeds of the Kingdom, which literally caused Christ to be formed in them.

As the prophet Samuel and his successors prophesied into the future, they impregnated the atmosphere with the seed of God, which in turn created a kind of gestation in creation itself. That is why Romans says, "For we know that the whole creation groans and suffers the pains of childbirth together until now" (Romans 8:22). Jesus spoke of world tribulation that would take place at the *end of the age*, saying, "But all these things are merely the beginning of birth pangs" (Matthew 24:8). Creation itself is in labor as it is giving birth to the heirs of salvation. The head is crowning just in time; the world, groaning in the hope of redemption, will be delivered from this present darkness.

The Israel of God

Before we uncover some of the prophetic declarations that have impregnated the cosmos, it is important that we understand that most of the promises, proclamations and prophecies that were made over Israel belong to the entire Body of Christ, not just to those born of natural Jewish descent. Paul said that Jesus had reconciled the Gentiles, who were once strangers to the *promises*, into one body, blending us with natural Jewish believers through the cross (see Ephesians 2:11–16). The promises are the fruit of the prophetic declarations God made through the Old Testament prophets.

Paul went on to say that the Spirit creates Jews through the circumcision of the heart, not by birthplace, genealogies or the efforts of men:

> For he is not a Jew who is one outwardly, nor is circumcision that which is outward in the flesh. But he is a Jew who is one inwardly; and circumcision is that which is of the heart, by the Spirit, not by the letter.
>
> Romans 2:28–29

> It is not the children of the flesh who are children of God, but the children of the promise are regarded as descendants.
>
> Romans 9:8

Writing to the believers in Rome, many of whom were Gentiles, Paul said, "For whatever was written in earlier times was written for our instruction, so that through perseverance and the encouragement of the Scriptures we might have hope" (Romans 15:4). This implies that what was written in the Old Testament was penned for the benefit of all believers, not just those born of Jewish origin.

Paul went on to make some radical statements to the Galatians, telling them, "Neither is circumcision anything, nor uncircumcision, but a new creation. And those who will walk by this rule, peace and mercy be upon them, and upon the Israel of God" (Galatians 6:15–16). He also said, "The Jerusalem above is free; she is our mother" (Galatians 4:26). Christians, both Jew and Gentile, are the Israel of God, and the New Jerusalem is our mother, our place of origin. Thus, although it is evident that some of the Old Testament promises have single-dimensional fulfillment in the nation of natural-born Israel alone, it is also evident that most of them have powerful secondary ramifications for all Christians. We are not trying to steal natural Israel's promises; we are simply borrowing them eternally as a part of the adopted cosmic family of God.

Becoming the Proclamations

Let's look at a few of the prophetic declarations, promises and provisions God has given us. He spoke to Abraham about a time when his descendants would benefit *all* the nations of the earth, saying, "I will multiply your descendants as the stars of heaven, and will give your descendants all these lands; and by your descendants all the nations of the earth shall be blessed" (Genesis 26:4). The birth of Christ in the lineage of Abraham initiated the fulfillment of this promise, but I am sure it is obvious that this declaration still lingers in the halls of history as the world waits for it to be fulfilled in the Body of Christ.

Ezekiel looked into the future and prophesied about a people who would have a new heart and a new spirit: "Moreover, I will give you a new heart and put a new spirit within you; and I will remove the heart of stone from your flesh and give you a heart of flesh" (Ezekiel 36:26). This is why the person who is least in the Kingdom of God is superior to John the Baptist, who was the greatest Old Testament prophet ever to set foot on this planet (see Matthew 11:11).

The prophet Zechariah spoke of a people who were so great that the feeblest among them would be like King David, and the house of David would be like God Himself (see Zechariah 12:8). Maybe that is why Jesus promised, "He who believes in Me, the works that I do, he will do also; and greater works than these he will do; because I go to the Father" (John 14:12).

The writer of Hebrews grabbed this Old Testament prophecy out of the book of Jeremiah and pulled it into the New Covenant:

> "They will not teach again, each man his neighbor and each man his brother, saying, 'Know the LORD,' for they will all know Me, from the least of them to the greatest of them," declares the LORD, "for I will forgive their iniquity, and their sin I will remember no more."
>
> Jeremiah 31:34; see also Hebrews 8:11–12

Just imagine, envision and dream about a time when everyone knows the Lord because He has inscribed His words on their hearts. Here is one of my favorite prophecies in the entire Bible:

> Now it will come about that in the last days the mountain of the house of the LORD will be established as the chief of the mountains, and will be raised above the hills; and all the nations will stream to it. And many peoples will come and say, "Come, let us go up to the mountain of the LORD, to the house of the God of Jacob; that He may teach us concerning His ways and that we may walk in His paths." For the law will go forth from Zion and the word of the LORD from Jerusalem. And He will judge between the nations, and will render decisions for many peoples; and they will hammer their swords into plowshares and their spears into pruning hooks. Nation will not lift up sword against nation, and never again will they learn war.
>
> Isaiah 2:2–4

Meditate on those verses for a while and they will make you happy! Nations will no longer be at war with each other because they are going to come to the house of the Lord and learn God's ways. Could this result, for example, in nations remodeling their weapons plants into factories that generate fresh produce to feed the world? It totally makes sense when you compare Isaiah's prophecy with the commission that Jesus gave us to make disciples of *all nations* and then teach them everything He taught us (see Matthew 28:19–20). This could be one of the ways that we are to be a blessing to all the countries in the world.

This is, in effect, a process of "pro-creation" at work. There are hundreds of verses that Samuel and his successors prophesied concerning us. It would take an entire book just to investigate a few of them. But my purpose here is simply to point out how God turns history into *His*-story. The Lord gives His prophets and prophetic people timeless insights. These history makers take these insights and proclaim them into the cosmos, impregnating the atmosphere with destiny and purpose. These prophetic words become catalytic agents that mold the events of our lives, personally and corporately, into a beautiful tapestry of historic exploits. The outcome is that these hidden mysteries that lie deep in the heart of the Father begin to be painted on the canvas of time.

Running Out of Time

Let's fast-forward again to the year 1970, when a dramatic shift took place in our worldview. Hal Lindsey published his book *The Late Great Planet Earth* (Zondervan). This book helped popularize an eschatology that changed the Church's message from "the Kingdom is at hand" to "the end of the world is near." It assisted in creating an expectation that the Antichrist would soon institute the destructive nature of "the Beast" and his deceptive mark.

This resulted in a kind of "Beam me up, Scotty" theology in most Christians as we began to anticipate a sudden cosmic rescue. (Let me be clear that Hal Lindsey, the author of the book, simply put words to an end-time view that was already popular in the Jesus movement. And like all of us in every epoch season, he was operating out of the revelation revealed to his generation.) One of the main verses shouted in this eschatology was, "But woe to them that are with child, and to them that give suck in those days!" (Mark 13:17 KJV). Was it a coincidence that three years after this book was published, *Roe v. Wade* passed the Supreme Court and it became legal to take the life of our unborn in every state in America? Is it possible that many misguided people considered abortion some sort of mercy killing? Could it be that some people could not bear the thought of bringing children into a world where the Antichrist would make them take a number or would torture them into compliance?

You might be asking, "Where was the Church during these crucial Supreme Court proceedings?" I will tell you where: We were waiting for the Rapture. Our eschatology taught us that there was not supposed to be a future. Personally, I never went to college because I did not want to "waste my time" on something that was "all going to burn," as we commonly used to say.

Here is another interesting side note: I was born January 31, 1955, the same year that Steve Jobs and Bill Gates were born. And Bill Joy was born in November 1954. These men were some of the main catalysts who birthed the Information Age. Few, if any, of the people who ushered in the Information Age were followers of Jesus Christ. Steve Jobs was a Buddhist, Bill Gates is an agnostic, Michael Dell is Jewish, and I am not sure about Bill Joy.

"So what's the point?" you ask. Have you ever wondered why there was hardly a single Christian at the forefront of the emerging Information Age? I believe it is because the Jesus movement, which largely embraced the *Late Great* eschatology, was birthed at the same time. Christian young people were all waiting for the great escape, leaving their non-Christian peers to follow the *kairos* clock of the Information Age and become the forerunners of the new epoch season. There were no Christian forerunners because there were no forethinkers. We were all taught to live for eternity, but no one seemed to understand that we were also supposed to live *from* eternity.

Someone Hijacked History

By now you are probably saying, "Kris, what the heck are you talking about?" Let me explain. Could it be that the worst element of this end-time paradigm is that it helps empower a dethroned devil to steal our children's future? Remember what I shared with you in the beginning of this chapter? The way that God creates history is by anointing people to see the future from His perspective and call it into existence (see Romans 4:17). Then, like Josiah and Peter, the people of each generation step into their destiny by fulfilling the words that were prophesied over them in the past.

But part of each generation's destiny is to keep the voice of the Lord alive by prophesying destiny over the generations to come. Just as Jesus said to the apostle John, "Come up here, and I will show you what must take place after these things" (Revelation 4:1), God invites us to sit with Him in heavenly places, where we can see from His perspective what He wants to take place in the future. It is from this posture that we can prophesy *from eternity*, because we received foresight and insight that is being empowered by *His*-sight. Our words become worlds, and history is transformed into *His*-story. Thus, we become the answers to the prayers and prophecies of Samuel and his successors, and we also join the ranks of successors by releasing our own prayers and prophecies over our future generations.

But what happened to destiny when our prophetic people were taught that there was not supposed to be a future because the end of the world was near? They stopped prophesying into the future. And what took place in the absence of the Holy Spirit's prophetic intonation is absolutely frightening. A visionary vortex or vacuum was suddenly created that sucked every kind of dark foretelling spirit into it. This has resulted in the worst psychic resurgence since the days of Daniel. We have Wiccans, New Age people, fortune-tellers, astrologers and psychics all sharing their insights in some of the highest offices in our land. It has become an accepted practice to employ these demonically anointed people to help prevent crimes and solve problems. The Department of Homeland Security, the FBI, the CIA and even our local police forces are all employing them. Of course, it is not hard for psychics to have insight into the crimes that their boss has plotted, planned and inspired.

Not only is a vacuum of true prophetic declarations creating a crisis in history, but our enemy has also taken over our abandoned role of declaring destiny and is perpetuating his diabolical schemes on our planet. As long as we shirk our commission to destroy the works of the devil, we fail to arrest his mission to kill, steal and destroy (see John 10:10; 1 John 3:8).

Our Legacy

We must consider the fact that our eschatology could be robbing us of our legacy. Remember, "The secret things belong to the LORD our God, but the things revealed belong to us and to our sons forever" (Deuteronomy 29:29). Prophetic revelation unlocks the hidden treasures that are to be handed down from generation to generation. But in order for us to prophesy the future and thus lay a foundation for a multigenerational inheritance, we must believe that there is supposed to be a future.

In the winter of 2007, the Lord spoke to me, saying, *The spirit of fatalism and the spirit of martyrdom are holding back the apostolic age.*

Fatalism refuses to acknowledge positive advancement on the earth and looks for the world to erode instead of evolve. It forces Scriptures such as "There will be no end to the increase of His government or of peace" (Isaiah 9:7) into a distant future that prevents them from inspiring hope for the coming generations.

The Church is notorious for using fear as a primary motivator to urge people to come into the Kingdom. We need to make sure that we don't build a partnership with terrorist spirits, believing we can drive people to God that way. There is no fear in love, and it is actually the kindness of God that leads us to repentance (see Romans 2:4). It is very difficult to keep people in the Kingdom who have been driven there predominantly by a fatalist eschatology.

Fatalistic martyrdom embraces death in a sadistic way and values the cross above the joy set before us. Jesus *endured* the cross; He did not enjoy it. When it was His time to die, He even prayed, "Father, if You are willing, remove this cup from Me" (Luke 22:42).

An Apostolic Eschatology

The Lord went on to tell me that He was going to give us an "apostolic eschatology." In some earlier chapters, we explored the mission of a true apostle. I talked about the fact that apostolic ministry is synonymous with cultural transformation. We know that the only prayer Jesus ever taught us to pray includes the phrase that the Kingdom would come "on earth as it is in heaven." Therefore, the first question we have to ask ourselves is this: *Did Jesus teach us to pray a prayer that He never intended us to believe?*

I think we can agree that the answer to that question is no. If we are to pray that it would be on earth as it is in heaven, and if we are commissioned to "make disciples of all the nations" (Matthew 28:19), then doesn't it stand to reason that we need a new approach to the end times?

What we believe about the end has a lot to do with how we behave in the middle. For example, say I have a 1955 Chevy and you have an automotive restoration shop. Imagine that I bring my car into your shop to be rebuilt from the ground up, and I inform you that money is no object. But in the middle of the restoration project, you discover that I plan to enter the old Chevy in a demolition derby after you complete the project. That information is definitely going to affect the quality of your work.

In the same way, any reasonable person should be able to figure out that holding a particular end-time perspective can dramatically affect the quality of his or her daily life. Once again, Isaiah prophesied that the Spirit of the Lord has anointed us to see freedom and restoration come into people's lives and described how *their* personal restoration would result in cities and nations being rebuilt. He wrote, "Then they will rebuild the ancient ruins, they will raise up the former devastations; and they will repair the ruined cities, the desolations of many generations" (Isaiah 61:4).

It is difficult to feel empowered to restore ruined cities and at the same time believe that the condition of the world needs to erode in order for Jesus to return. Can you see that our eschatology is actually working against our ministry? Jack Taylor of Dimensions Ministries put it this way: "It's hard to give people heaven by the half acre while believing that things are going to hell in a handbasket." I wonder if it is possible that we are actually on the eve of construction?

The Plight of Creation Care

This point was brought to my mind again recently when I was invited to a roundtable summit where several hundred leaders gathered to discuss the diverse challenges of cultural transformation. The purpose of the conference was to find creative solutions for the world's problems. The event was divided into several topics we had the privilege of dialoguing about. Ecology, or Creation Care, was one of the main themes of our discussion.

Different leaders passionately debated the subject of ecology as several of us listened attentively. One speaker pointed out that cultivating the planet was the first responsibility that God gave to Adam personally and the second command He gave to man corporately (see Genesis 1:20–31; 2:15).[1] Another individual expounded on the fact that the New Age movement is leading the Green Revolution and that Christians are decades behind the rest of the world on the subject. That comment inspired a couple of hours of dialogue as several bright Christian scientists and ecologists weighed in on the matter.

As the dialogue went on, I had this thought: *There is an elephant in the room, and nobody wants to talk about it. Our eschatology seems to be undermining our ecology.* The planet, metaphorically speaking, is our '55 Chevy, and the Church is God's restoration shop. We are bringing our discussions about the stewardship of the planet into Church with us these days, but all the while we are looking for its "any minute now" destruction. It is hard to get excited about restoring something that we think is about to go up in flames. Peter put it like this:

> Therefore repent and return, so that your sins may be wiped away, in order that times of refreshing may come from the presence of the Lord; and that He may send Jesus, the Christ appointed for you, whom heaven must receive until the period of

restoration of all things about which God spoke by the mouth of His holy prophets from ancient time.

Acts 3:19–21

As I have mentioned several times already, we are called to bring heaven to earth and thus become catalysts for the restoration of all things. But it is hard to get excited about the ministry of restoration or the promise of the meek inheriting the earth while envisioning a Cajun-cooked planet.

Light and Darkness

For years, I preached that in the last days the light is going to get brighter and brighter, while the darkness gets darker and darker. Then one day I had this revelation: Light and darkness cannot cohabit. It is scientifically impossible to increase the light in a room and have it simultaneously get darker—unless you shield the light with something. The only other way to have light and darkness intensify concurrently is to confine or limit the light to a certain geographic or demographic location. But Jesus said,

> You are the light of the world. A city set on a hill cannot be hidden; nor does anyone light a lamp and put it under a basket, but on the lampstand, and it gives light to all who are in the house. Let your light shine before men in such a way that they may see your good works, and glorify your Father who is in heaven.
>
> Matthew 5:14–16

Jesus made it clear that we are the light of the entire *world*. We are supposed to place our light in the highest, most visible location possible in each of our cities. It is never to be hidden under a basket or shielded by an object. If this is true, then it should inspire many questions in our hearts. For example, what about all the verses in the New Testament that speak about the terrible times that are coming in the last days?

Good question. Let's talk about a few possible explanations. For one thing, we have to understand that the phrase "the last days" spans thousands of years, beginning with Peter's proclamation from the prophet Joel in Acts 2:17 and extending to the return of Jesus. The Bible refers to several different kinds of events, as well as to various epoch season changes taking place in the midst of this timeline called the last days. Some of them are very bad and dark, while others are amazing and full of light. We have, for example, Scriptures like 2 Timothy 3:1–5, where Paul writes to instruct his disciple on how he should respond to evil people in the last days:

> But realize this, that in the last days difficult times will come. For men will be lovers of self, lovers of money, boastful, arrogant, revilers, disobedient to parents, ungrateful, unholy, unloving, irreconcilable, malicious gossips, without self-control, brutal, haters of good, treacherous, reckless, conceited, lovers of pleasure rather than lovers of God, holding to a form of godliness, although they have denied its power; avoid such men as these.

The real question is, where do these verses belong in the timeline of "the last days"? A couple of things come to mind. First, it is clear that Paul expected Timothy to experience these things in his day. He gives him *personal* instruction about how to deal with people bent on evil. In other words, he was not necessarily giving Timothy a commentary on the condition of the planet at the return of Jesus; he could have been exhorting him about the days in which they currently lived. So my question is, when we see people in this evil condition living around us, does it really prove that things are getting worse?

In order to understand the full counsel of God when we are developing an end-time mindset, we must embrace all Scriptures that deal with the last days, like this one in the book of Isaiah:

> Arise, shine; for your light has come, and the glory of the LORD has risen upon you. For behold, darkness will cover the earth and deep darkness the peoples; but the LORD will rise upon you and His glory will appear upon you. Nations will come to your light, and kings to the brightness of your rising. Lift up your eyes round about and see; they all gather together, they come to you. Your sons will come from afar, and your daughters will be carried in the arms. Then you will see and be radiant, and your heart will thrill and rejoice; because the abundance of the sea will be turned to you, the wealth of the nations will come to you.
>
> Isaiah 60:1–5

Notice that God exhorts us to arise in the midst of the deep darkness that is upon the people and begin to shine. This positive posture of arising results in nations, kings and people coming from around the world to be healed, saved, delivered and transformed. Their condition is so desperate that they are willing to offer all their wealth to the people of God in exchange for their darkened condition becoming enlightened.

I think that Scriptures like Paul's exhortation to Timothy could be a perfect description of the deep darkness that the Church has been commanded to arise and shine in. Is it possible that the outcome of the Body of Christ shining in the midst of the worst conditions on the planet is not that evil somehow increases, but that it is destroyed?

End-Time Thoughts

It would take an entire book to do any justice to the subject of the end times. Harold Eberle and Martin Trench have written a great book titled *Victorious Eschatology* (Worldcast Publishing, 2007). They have some fresh perspectives and real insights into the Scriptures dealing with this subject. I recommend that you read their book with an open mind. It covers Jesus' "end of the age" prophecy in Matthew 24 and also gives a refreshing perspective on the book of Revelation. For whatever it is worth, their book did not inspire this chapter. I have held this positive eschatological view for many years. It was, however, inspiring for me to find other leaders who share a victorious understanding of the last days.

The goal of this book is not to give you another chart to argue over or to enter into a theological debate on the various views of end-time prophecy. I simply want to challenge your thinking. I want you to be aware that, like it or not, your eschatological core values could be affecting your ministry, and more importantly, your legacy. We owe it to our children's children's children to have the courage to question old paradigms that could rob hope from the coming generations. Hope is the seedbed that faith grows in, and faith is what Jesus is looking for when He returns to the planet: "When the Son of Man comes, will He find faith on the earth?" (Luke 18:8).

Bill Johnson says, "To think that things are going to get worse and worse in the last days takes no faith." What is more, desiring that Jesus returns right now relegates billions of people to hell. Peter understood this when he said, "The Lord is not slow about His promise, as some count slowness, but is patient toward you, not wishing for any to perish but for all to come to repentance" (2 Peter 3:9).

It is so important that we put on the mind of Christ and not let our *circumstances* dictate our *stances*. Every time we react to the world's condition instead of responding in faith, we find ourselves *under* the circumstances. A lot of bad doctrine comes out of a sense of powerless Christianity. We tend to spiritualize our dysfunction, mask our fears and excuse our inability to see greater works happen through our lives.

Personally, I am on an eschatological journey. I feel like Abram when he first met God. The Lord told him to leave his country and journey to a land He would show him (see Genesis 12:1). Abram did not know where he was going; he just knew where he could not stay. I know I cannot stay in the end-time theology that is stealing my children's future, instilling fear as a primary motivation for serving the Father and undermining the Great Commission to make disciples of *all* nations.

Even though I am not sure where I am going, I have decided to allow a few simple core values to determine my eschatological journey. First, I will not let mystical passages that have been debated for centuries undermine the clear commands, promises and prophecies we have from the Lord Himself, many of which I have already discussed at length in these pages. Second, I will not embrace an end-time view that diminishes hope, promotes fear or re-arms the same devil whom Jesus disarmed on the cross (see Colossians 2:13–15).

The book of Revelation was written to be the revelation of Jesus Christ, not the revelation of the Antichrist (see Revelation 1:1). It was penned in a prophetic style common to the mystics; therefore, it is prone to subjectivity. I will not allow its interpretation to promote powerless Christianity.

The command that has been passed down from generation to generation with growing momentum is to destroy the works of the devil (see 1 John 3:8). It remains true in every epoch season in life that when we submit to God and resist the devil, he flees from us (see James 4:7). I will not embrace an eschatology that undermines our commission to make disciples of all nations or deters our mandate to restore our ruined cities.

Finally, I will not believe any end-time interpretation of Scripture that redefines the nature of God. He is good all the time.

His love for us is indescribable, incomprehensible, unimaginable and impossible to exaggerate. His mercy runs deeper than the ocean, His compassion is wider than the sea, and His thoughts toward us are innumerable. He created us for His pleasure and therefore enjoys being with us.

With all that being said, there are still Scriptures that seem to point to another perspective that is highly pessimistic and cannot be ignored. As a result, it is my conviction that more than ever, we need the Holy Spirit to lead us into all truth and guide us through these theological minefields in our eschatological journey. May God give us wisdom and insight for the times that we live in, and may we together find the Promised Land of our souls.

16

::

It's a Wonderful World

Sometimes things that are too good to be true are true!

Anonymous

In 1967, Louis Armstrong, an African American basking in the fresh flame of the civil rights movement, stared down the doomsayers of his era when he sang the famous song "What a Wonderful World." In the song, he sang about trees of green, and red roses, too, blooming "for me and you," and he thought to himself about "what a wonderful world" it is.[1] A couple of years ago, I downloaded the song onto my iPod and happened to listen to it for the first time during a flight on my way to a conference. The song unearthed a crisis in my soul, one so deep that I was unaware it even existed. As the song played, I found myself in a battle that is impossible to explain accurately with mere words, but I will try. My heart wrenched with every line of the lyrics as my mind engaged in a heated conflict within itself. My brain became a battlefield, and various Scriptures emerged as soldiers warring against one another in a kind of noble struggle for truth.

I kept pushing replay on my iPod, because it felt as though Louis's words were reinforcements in my war for reality. As the hours passed, I came to understand that a foreboding spirit (foreboding means an impending sense of doom) had somehow lodged itself in my soul and was dictating my worldview. I realized that there was some sort of warped need in me to believe that things were getting worse in the world.

Yet there I was, flying halfway around the world on a twelve-hour flight aboard an air-conditioned jet, thousands of miles from home. I was making a journey that only a century ago would have taken a year on horseback or many months on a ship, and would have been incalculably more dangerous.

The war in my mind intensified, so I decided to retreat to a movie for a couple of hours of solace. I adjusted the TV screen in front of me and began to check out the selection. As I flipped through the choices, I was frustrated that they seemed a bit dated. I had already watched most of the ten movies the airline offered. The other shows were chick flicks, and I was not desperate enough to cry through a movie for entertainment. I grumbled to myself about how badly the financial crisis had affected the transportation industry. But just then, I remembered that I had brought a DVD with me. I opened my laptop, put my Bose noise-canceling headset on and inserted the movie.

By now all this stress was giving me the munchies, so I pushed the button to alert the flight attendant that I needed her attention. She came over to my seat and just happened to have my favorite soda in her cart. I asked her for something to eat. She showed me a menu and informed me that I would have to pay five dollars for a meal.

"Five dollars!" I whined. "What's happening to this world?"

She explained that things were really tough in the airline business, so they had to start charging for stuff they used to give away. I moaned a little more, pulled out my American Express card and charged the meal.

When we finally landed, I called Kathy on my cell phone to let her know I had arrived safely. We talked for a while and she informed me that the water district had raised our rates 20 percent due to the severe drought conditions that were hammering Northern California. She went on to suggest that we cut back on watering our lawn.

"I want our lawn to stay green," I protested. When we hung up the phone, I thought to myself, *Global warming is already killing my lawn!*

My host was at the baggage claim to pick me up when I arrived. It was really hot outside, but he had kept the car running so that the vehicle would be a cool 70 degrees when I got in. He asked if I had been able to sleep on my twelve-hour international flight.

"No," I complained. "It was a hard flight. I had to ride in the cattle car seats."

We stopped at Starbucks to get a $4 cup of coffee on the way to our hotel. As he drove, I pulled out *USA Today* and began to read. The bad news regarding the more than seven billion people who inhabit this planet filled several pages of the paper. I felt terrible for Tiger Woods's family as the story of his affairs, which had been unfolding for days, continued, taking up several columns. *Wow,* I thought, *what's this world coming to?*

We finally arrived at the conference, where two thousand people were waiting in a beautiful sanctuary complete with deeply padded chairs. An anointed worship team led us in adoration of the Lord, their voices mixed to perfection on a $30,000 soundboard and delivered to us through a state-of-the-art sound system.

Soon it was my turn to speak. "The world is getting darker and darker as we progress through these last days," I proclaimed. But something did not seem right about that statement anymore. I struggled in my soul, feeling as if I were being dishonest with the congregation. It was then I realized that the soldiers of truth that had been waging war on the battlefield of my mind had somehow challenged my worldview.

It might just be time to face some of the terrible truth about the improving state of the world. I began to question reality, and I wondered where I had picked up these negative mindsets while living in a level of luxury that kings had not known a mere century ago.

Dark Glasses

As I pondered these things, I came to recognize that I was born into a world darkened in understanding. Although I was enlightened to the truth of salvation by faith, I had somehow chosen to leave the dark glasses of doubt on when viewing the Lord's parish, the world that He loves so much. After all, such sunglasses were in vogue—everybody was wearing them, and I did not want the Christian crowd to reject me.

I have also since come to recognize that bad news sells. The average person today hears more negative reports in one week than someone just fifty years ago would have heard in a lifetime. I began to understand that the world has satisfied its appetite for bad news by developing tracking systems that report what is wrong in the world instead of what is right. For example, we track the unemployment rate, not the employment rate. Think about the mindset that develops from focusing on the fact that 12 percent of our nation's workforce is unemployed instead of the fact that 88 percent of Americans are working (at the time of this writing). So many statistics are designed to gauge what is wrong with humanity instead of what is right.

Bad news is so popular that the media has even figured out a way to negatively report good news. Gas prices are a great example. When the average price of gas rose to more than $2 a gallon in June 2008, the news reports spoke of the evils of hyperinflation. Later, when the price dropped to an average of $1.61 per gallon in December, the media headlines thundered "The Economic Ills of Deflation."

I am not trying to bury my head in the sand and pretend there are no serious problems in the world. Nor am I advocating living in a fantasy world of denial and calling it faith. But I will not relegate my worldview to lies so that I can somehow rejoice over the fulfillment of some "end-time" verse in the Bible. God wants us to embrace the truth, not popular opinion.

Good News Is Hard to Believe

There has been so much good news on this planet in the last one hundred years that it is hard to comprehend why it is not on the front page of every newspaper in the country. Thankfully, Stephen Moore and Julian L. Simon have gone through the trouble of compiling many of these neglected facts in one volume called *It's Getting Better All the Time: 100 Greatest Trends of the Last 100 Years* (Cato Institute, 2000). I would like to share just a sampling of their findings here that show how the world is improving rather than declining.

Health

We have now completely eradicated from the globe diseases that for decades wiped out entire civilizations. Smallpox, for example, is nothing more than a history lesson now studied in textbooks that elementary school children read.

For much of human history, a person's average life expectancy was between 20 and 30 years. By 2003, the average person worldwide lived to be nearly 67 years old, and life expectancy is still rising.[2] Even in Africa, the poorest continent in the world, it has increased to 46 years old.[3]

But wait; there is more good news. Not only are people living longer today; they are also healthier in their old age. People get sick much later in life. For example, people contract heart disease at least nine years later than they did just a century ago. Respiratory diseases have been delayed an average of eleven years, and cancer eight years.[4]

Before industrialization, at least one in five children died before reaching his or her first birthday. By 2003, the worldwide infant mortality rate had dropped by nearly 75 percent, to one in every seventeen children.[5]

While we are on the subject of health, let's talk about smoking. In 1965, approximately one of every two people smoked in America. By the year 2006, that number had dropped to about one in every five people.[6] In other words, in the last forty years or so, nearly 64 million people have quit smoking in the U.S. alone.

Pollution

Nearly half a century ago, doomsayer Paul Ehrlich wrote in his book *The Population Bomb* (Ballantine, 1968) that "smog disasters" might kill two hundred thousand people in New York City and Los Angeles alone by 1973.[7] But in reality, air pollution in American cities has been declining for the past three decades. Better air quality trends have not been confined to just a handful of cities, either. Over the 25-year period beginning in 1962 and ending in 1987, smog levels fell by more than half.[8]

Not only is air quality improving drastically; water quality is also improving. According to the Pacific Research Institutes *Index of Leading Environmental Indicators*, in 1972 only

36 percent of U.S. lakes were usable for fishing and swimming. By 1994, that number had risen to 91 percent.[9] And the percentage of water sources that were judged poor or severe by the Council on Environmental Quality fell from 30 percent in 1961 to less than 5 percent today.[10]

Poverty

The average person has never been better fed than he or she is today. Between 1961 and 2002, the world's average daily food supply increased by 24 percent per person (38 percent in developing nations). The chronic undernourishment in developing nations declined from 37 percent to 17 percent of their population in that same period.[11] Since 1950, inflation-adjusted prices of food commodities have declined by 75 percent because of greater agricultural productivity and international trade. At the same time, access to safe water and sanitation has increased dramatically.[12]

Abortion

In spite of all the "pro-choice" media pressure leveled at society, abortion rates are tumbling. According to the Guttmacher Institute's 2005 survey of abortion providers, the abortion rate declined 25 percent during the last fifteen years in the United States.[13] That equates to four hundred thousand fewer babies aborted in America alone in 2005 than there were in 1990. The good news is that the abortion rate is still dropping drastically.

Let me make it clear that abortion is still the most serious crime ever committed against humanity, and millions of children are still being aborted here and abroad. We need to continue the struggle for the unborn until abortion is ancient history, like smallpox. But what I am pointing out is that we can see clear movement in that direction.

Population Growth

Decreasing abortion rates, longer life expectancy, reduced infant deaths, major decreases in starvation and the overall improving state of the planet have resulted in the world's population growing quite dramatically. At the turn of the twentieth century, for example, the population of the earth was about 1.6 billion. Today there are more than 7.4 billion people gracing this planet. More people lived on the earth in this last century than have been born in all of previous history combined. Experts say that by 2050 there will be 9 billion people living on this planet.[14] What is exciting about this is that behind every number is a person made in God's image.

Civil Rights

Let's look at some other areas of social and moral progress, like civil rights. When we think of the oppression of women in countries like Afghanistan, we often forget that until August 26, 1920, women in America could not even vote. After thousands of years of oppression and domination by men, women are finally winning back their God-given place in society. When God created humankind, both male and female, He commissioned them both to take dominion over the planet (see Genesis 1:26–28). Men were never given authority over women until the Fall in the Garden. Contrary to popular opinion, male domination was part of the curse, not part of the original order of creation (see Genesis 3:16).

Jesus was crucified to deliver all of creation from the curse. Two thousand years later, women all over the world are beginning to experience the freedom that their Savior purchased for them on the cross. Women are finding their way into the marketplace in record numbers. They are emerging as incredible leaders in business, education, politics and every walk of life and field of employment. Even the Body of Christ is realizing our need for female leadership and commissioning women to help govern our churches. Go, ladies!

A discussion about American civil rights would not be complete without recounting the African-American struggle for freedom and equality. From 1654 until 1863, slavery was legal within the boundaries of much of the present United States. It was only after the bloodiest war in American history that Abraham Lincoln's Emancipation Proclamation freed black people from slavery, though the struggle for freedom went on long after the legal battle had been won. The Fifteenth Amendment to the Constitution granted African-American men the right to vote by declaring that the "right of citizens of the United States to vote shall not be denied or abridged by the United States or by any state on account of race, color, or previous condition of servitude." Although ratified on February 3, 1870, the promise of the Fifteenth Amendment would not be fully realized for almost a century.

Again, the civil rights movement of the sixties, stimulated by Rosa Parks and led by Dr. Martin Luther King Jr., continued the struggle of equality for African-American citizens. Dr. King gave his life fighting for equal rights for people of all colors. Watching President Obama take the oath of the highest office in our land had to be the ultimate climax in African-American history so far. Even if you did not vote for him, you can still feel a sense of poetic justice in his presidency.

Freedom to Vote

Ever since the women's rights movement and the civil rights movement, most Americans take the right to vote for granted. But back in 1900, not one country had universal suffrage (the right for all its adult citizens to vote), and only 12.4 percent of the world's population had even limited suffrage. Today, 44.1 percent of the world's people live in nations deemed free by Freedom House, and another 18.6 percent live in nations deemed partly free.[15]

Spiritual Hunger

Throughout this chapter we have discussed just a little bit of the good news taking place in our world today, but we have yet to even touch on the positive spiritual movements of our times. Did you know that more people are finding Christ today than at any other time in human history?

Do you realize that many places once dominated by atheism, Islam and Buddhism are now experiencing incredible revivals? The intense spiritual hunger in China, Africa and Russia, for example, is causing unprecedented revival.

In our own Bethel movement, we literally see hundreds of healings, miracles, salvations and divine interventions of God every month.

Is the World Eroding or Evolving?

With all this good news, why think things are getting worse? Why are people convinced that the world is eroding rather than evolving? First, you have to find out who is carrying this negative message. Do you suppose that any open-minded person actually believes the world is getting worse for women? How about for African Americans? How would they answer the question of whether or not their race is worse off today than it was a hundred years ago? Are the Russians better off today than they were under Communism? Or was the world a better place under the tyranny of Hitler, Stalin and Saddam Hussein?

If the believers who are least in the Kingdom of God are superior to the greatest prophet who ever lived under the Old Covenant (John the Baptist; see Matthew 11:11), then at least we know that folks who receive Christ today are better off than they were in ancient times. And if Christ died to disarm the devil and gave all His authority to His Church, then we would have to conclude that the world is better off than it was before Christ's victory on the cross (see Colossians 2:13–15; Ephesians 1:18–23).

"All right," you say, "I concede. But you're missing the point! You're ignoring the major sin issues of our time. How about murder, homosexuality, the cults and the occult? Aren't they taking over our world?"

Think about it for a minute. The first murder took place with only four people on the planet, so when Cain killed Abel the murder rate instantly rose to 25 percent. And contrary to popular opinion, homosexuality did not begin in San Francisco; it is reported in the Bible. It was so prevalent that we get one of our names for sexual perversion, sodomy, from a biblical town (Sodom).

Further, do you believe that political corruption was initiated at Watergate? Have you ever read the story of David (the man after God's own heart) and his adulterous relationship with Bathsheba, which included the murder of her husband, Uriah? Do you realize that 80 percent of all of Israel's kings listed in the Bible were wicked?

Do you think that false religions began with the New Age movement? Have you missed reading all the accounts in the Old Testament of Baal worship and the children who were sacrificed on his altars? Are you aware that the psychics of today were the satraps of Daniel's day? Do you believe that Greek mythology is any less destructive than Mormonism, Jehovah's Witnesses or Islam? Maybe the good old days were not quite as wonderful as we like to recount them.

But the World Is More Dangerous. . . .

"Well, okay," you say, "but isn't it true that with the invention of the atomic bomb, the world is a much more dangerous place?"

The answer to that question is yes . . . and no. Of course, even an idiot has to acknowledge that for the first time in history, mankind literally has the capacity to destroy the planet. If some nut starts a nuclear war, all the facts in this chapter *could* instantly become irrelevant.

On the other hand, for centuries violent dictators have ravaged weaker countries, pillaging their people and destroying their cities. Tyrants like Alexander the Great, Julius Caesar, Adolph Hitler, Napoleon of France, Joseph Stalin, Vladimir Lenin and Genghis Khan were determined to rule the world by crushing their opposition with their military might. These men ruled their empires with an iron fist, committing unimaginable atrocities against their enemies and often terrorizing their own citizens.

But strangely, since the invention of the atomic bomb and the demonstration of its destructive ability, tyrants have been kept in check, knowing that their violent acts of aggression could very well result in their countries being blown off the map. And even if an oppressor possesses nuclear weapons, that arsenal is accompanied by the understanding that attacking another nation protected by the same kind of arsenal is a lose-lose situation. When the battle is over and the mushroom clouds finally dissipate, there would be nothing left to rule.

After Adolph Hitler tried to conquer the world, the nations were motivated to work together to stop tyrants and promote world peace. The United Nations was founded in 1945 on the premise of ensuring international security and protecting human rights. Although this young organization has not always fulfilled its professed mission very well (for example in Rwanda, where U.N. peacekeeping forces pulled out of the country during the genocide, thus allowing the slaughter of a million people in three months), it is a huge step forward in the process toward a better and safer world.

Antichrist Is Coming!

Even as I write this chapter, I am aware that a large number of Christians are convinced that any form of cooperative globalization is the beginning of the Antichrist's one-world government, which will be followed by the mark of the Beast and a climax in the battle of Armageddon. Are you aware that the idea of the Antichrist developing a one-world government is basically being taught on the basis of three Scripture passages? Here they are:

> In that you saw the feet and toes, partly of potter's clay and partly of iron, it will be a divided kingdom; but it will have in it the toughness of iron, inasmuch as you saw the iron mixed with common clay. As the toes of the feet were partly of iron and partly of pottery, so some of the kingdom will be strong and part of it will be brittle.
>
> Daniel 2:41–42

> I approached one of those who were standing by and began asking him the exact meaning of all this. So he told me and made known to me the interpretation of these things: "These great beasts, which are four in number, are four kings who will arise from the earth. But the saints of the Highest One will receive the kingdom and possess the kingdom forever, for all ages to come."
>
> Then I desired to know the exact meaning of the fourth beast, which was different from all the others, exceedingly dreadful, with its teeth of iron and its claws of bronze, and which devoured, crushed and trampled down the remainder with its feet, and the meaning of the ten horns that were on its head and the other horn which came up, and before which three of them fell, namely, that horn which had eyes and a mouth uttering great boasts and which was larger in appearance than its associates. I kept looking, and that horn was waging war with the saints and overpowering them until the Ancient of Days came and judgment was passed in favor

of the saints of the Highest One, and the time arrived when the saints took possession of the kingdom.

Thus he said: "The fourth beast will be a fourth kingdom on the earth, which will be different from all the other kingdoms and will devour the whole earth and tread it down and crush it. As for the ten horns, out of this kingdom ten kings will arise; and another will arise after them, and he will be different from the previous ones and will subdue three kings. He will speak out against the Most High and wear down the saints of the Highest One, and he will intend to make alterations in times and in law; and they will be given into his hand for a time, times, and half a time."

Daniel 7:16–25

And the dragon stood on the sand of the seashore.

Then I saw a beast coming up out of the sea, having ten horns and seven heads, and on his horns were ten diadems, and on his heads were blasphemous names. . . .

It was also given to him to make war with the saints and to overcome them, and authority over every tribe and people and tongue and nation was given to him.

Revelation 13:1, 7

Did you find the Antichrist's one-world government in these passages? Apparently you should have, because these are the main Scriptures that are causing thousands of Christians to resist nations working together for the common good of the global population. Is it just me, or do you think that someone would have to have a pretty good imagination (or a preconceived idea) to get a one-world Antichrist government out of these Scriptures? I have a struggle with believers who read their ideas into the Scriptures, especially in a way that undermines the Great Commission and subverts the Lord's Prayer.

Many Christians have developed a "damned if you do and damned if you don't" theological worldview. They are so convinced that things "must get worse" in order for Jesus to return that they have become marooned on a small island, lost somewhere between "You will be hearing of wars and rumors of wars" and "While they are saying, 'Peace and safety!' then destruction will come upon them suddenly" (Matthew 24:6; 1 Thessalonians 5:3).

If these two Scriptures make up your entire eschatological paradigm, then you basically have two boxes to put all your world news in. Bad news goes into the "everything needs to get worse" box, and good news gets sorted into the "if things look good, destruction is near" box.

If you only embrace a few portions of Scripture as the full counsel of God, how do you have any faith for the restoration of nations, for making disciples of *all* nations, for destroying the works of the devil and for doing greater works than Jesus did? (See Isaiah 6:41; Matthew 28:19; 1 John 3:8; John 14:12.)

What Is Real?

As I pointed out earlier, I am not claiming to have all the answers. I certainly do not. But I have found that people who think they have all the answers usually have misunderstood the questions.

The challenges we face today are complex, and they will never be solved by one person or answered in a single book. I believe, however, that wisdom comes as we define reality. Pilate asked Jesus, "What is truth?" (John 18:38). He was not asking Jesus, "What does the Bible say?" No, the Greek word for *truth* here means "real." Pilate was literally asking Jesus, "What is real?"

You cannot define reality until you have questioned it. I must admit that in these critical days in which we live, I often have found myself asking Jesus the same question Pilate asked when he was making the most important decision of his life (whether or not he should crucify Christ). Pilate finally got it right, but it was too late. The best he could do was wash his hands of the situation (see Matthew 27:24).

During the American Civil War, many devout Christians fought *for*—meaning in favor of—slavery. These believers took Scriptures like Paul's letter to the Colossians to mean that they had the God-given right to enslave people. They justified their position with verses like "Slaves, in all things obey those who are your masters on earth, not with external service, as those who merely please men, but with sincerity of heart, fearing the Lord," and "Masters, grant to your slaves justice and fairness, knowing that you too have a Master in heaven" (Colossians 3:22; 4:1). Sadly, they got it wrong, and 620,000 people died in the Civil War to set things right.

My Vision

I was lying on the floor of our prayer house in 2004, seeking God, when suddenly I was taken up in a vision that thrust me one hundred years into the future. I found myself standing next to an old man in the living room of a huge, ornate mansion. I could see him perfectly, but he could not see me. It felt as though it were Thanksgiving or something. The home was filled with the smells of pies baking in the oven, and the excitement of a large family gathering was in the air. The adults were talking and laughing as the kids played.

The elderly gentleman was encircled with several generations of family, all listening intently as he exuberantly told them stories and mused over the past, as old men often do. Then something happened. His tone changed and his face grew serious, as though he was about to share something of great importance with them. Tears formed in his eyes as he looked off into the distance, as though he was trying to recall some ancient secret told to him long ago. The entire room grew silent and more people gathered, leaning in to hear his every word.

He began to speak to those present about their noble roots and their royal heritage. He stared into the eyes of each one, as if he was looking for greatness in their souls. He spoke of the great price their forefathers had paid to obtain such favor, wealth and influence from God and man. But it was what he did next that stunned me. He pointed to a majestic stone fireplace that rose about thirty feet to a vaulted ceiling. I looked over toward the fireplace mantel, where a large, beautiful artist's portrait of Kathy and me hung. I was breathless as he finished his exhortation: "All this began with your great-great-great-grandmother and great-great-great-grandfather!"

I instantly came out of the vision, struggling to gather my thoughts. Next I heard a thundering voice speak to my spirit: *Your children's children's children are depending on you leaving them a world in revival. You are no longer to live for a ministry. From this day forward, you are to live to leave a legacy!*

There is a *heavy rain* coming that is about to saturate the entire planet. What will it look like when God pours His Spirit out on all flesh? This entire book has been dedicated to seeing and taking hold of God's vision for the future. We cannot afford to get this wrong. If we misinterpret God's heart for the future, it will be our children's children's children who will pay the greatest price for our mistake. On the other hand, if we get this right, we could be the catalysts to the greatest revival in the history of the world.

Let it rain!

Notes

Chapter 1: Re-forming the Church

1. Paul Manwaring is on the Senior Leadership Team at Bethel Church in Redding, California. He is founder of Global Legacy and oversees Bethel School of Supernatural Ministry's Third Year program, equipping and deploying revivalists. Paul speaks and preaches in venues around the world.

2. See Bethel Church's statement of faith at https://www.ibethel.org/about/.

Chapter 5: The Emerging Apostolic Age

1. American philosopher Eric Hoffer was awarded the Presidential Medal of Freedom in 1983. He called himself an atheist, but he also described religion as a positive force. His first book, *The True Believer: Thoughts on the Nature of Mass Movements*, published in 1951, is considered a classic.

Chapter 7: "Mr. Gorbachev, Tear Down This Wall!"

1. Mark Haefeli, director, *Paul McCartney in Red Square: A Concert Film* (A&E Home Video, 2003).

2. Frank Newport, "Americans Greatly Overestimate Percent Gay, Lesbian in U.S.," May 21, 2015, http://www.gallup.com/poll/183383/americans-greatly-over estimate-percent-gay-lesbian.aspx.

3. Jennifer Robison, "What Percentage of the Population Is Gay," Gallup, October 8, 2002. www.gallup.co/poll/6961/what-percentage-population-gay.aspx. Note that although this article is more than a decade old, the estimates have not changed much since that time. See http://www.thetaskforce.org/gallup-poll-finds -3-4-of-population-identify-as-lgbt/.

Chapter 8: Secret Agent Man

1. See the article "Cyrus Charter of the Human Rights Cylinder: First Charter of Human Rights," FarsiNet, © 1996–2016, http://www.farsinet.com/cyrus/.

Chapter 9: ISIS

1. Note that these two acronyms refer to the same group. ISIS stands for Islamic State in Iran and Syria. That group's territory straddles the border between the two countries. ISIL stands for Islamic State in Iraq and the Levant, with the Levant being the historic name given to the entire region east of the Mediterranean from Egypt, east to Iran and Turkey.

2. You can find this quote and more information on this topic in the article "What Does Islam Teach about . . . Violence," TheReligionofPeace, ©2002–2016, http://thereligionofpeace.com/pages/quran/violence.aspx.

3. Again, for more information on the jihadists and the Qur'an, visit The ReligionofPeace online at http://thereligionofpeace.com/pages/quran/violence.aspx.

Chapter 10: The Tipping Point

1. Malcolm Gladwell, *The Tipping Point: How Little Things Can Make a Big Difference* (New York: Back Bay Books, 2002), 28.

2. Quotes are taken from "Things That Will Never Happen," Rense.com, http://www.rense.com/general81/dw.htm.

3. John Lennon, "Imagine," from the album *Imagine* (London: Apple Records, 1971).

Chapter 11: Unreasonable Courage

1. This special excerpt called "The Man in the Arena" passage is from Theodore Roosevelt's speech "Citizenship in a Republic," which he delivered at the Sorbonne in Paris, France, on April 23, 1910.

2. Mick Jagger and Keith Richards, "(I Can't Get No) Satisfaction," *Out of Our Heads* (London: London Records, 1965).

Chapter 12: The Land of the Giants

1. Henrietta Elizabeth Marshall, *Scotland's Story: A History of Scotland for Boys and Girls* (London: Thomas Nelson and Sons Ltd., 1907), 185–187.

Chapter 14: Casting Vision and Capturing Hearts

1. Martin Luther King Jr. delivered his "I Have a Dream" speech from the steps of the Lincoln Memorial to more than 250,000 civil rights supporters on August 28, 1963, during the March on Washington for Jobs and Freedom.

2. King delivered his "I've Been to the Mountaintop" speech on April 3, 1968, at the Mason Temple (Church of God in Christ Headquarters) in Memphis, Tennessee.

Chapter 15: Impregnating the Cosmos

1. Note that the first corporate commission was, "Be fruitful and multiply" (Genesis 1:28).

Chapter 16: It's a Wonderful World

1. Bob Thiele and George David Weiss, "What a Wonderful World," performed by Louis Armstrong, © 1967 ABC Records.

2. Indur Goklany, *The Improving State of the World: Why We're Living Longer, Healthier, More Comfortable Lives on a Cleaner Planet* (Washington, D.C.: Cato Institute, 2007), 31.

3. Ibid., 69.

4. Ibid., 40.

5. Ibid., 27.

6. "Cigarette Smoking Among Adults—United States, 2006," *Morbidity and Mortality Weekly Report*, Centers for Disease Control and Prevention, November 9, 2007, http://www.cdc.gov/mmwr/preview/mmwrhtml/mm5644a2.htm#fig.

7. Stephen Moore and Julian L. Simon, *It's Getting Better All the Time: 100 Greatest Trends of the Last 100 Years* (Washington, D.C.: Cato Institute, 2000), 186.

8. Ibid.

9. Ibid., 188.

10. Ibid.

11. Goklany, *The Improving State of the World*, 21.

12. Ibid., 43–44.

13. Rachel K. Jones, Mia R. S. Zolna, Stanley K. Henshaw, and Lawrence B. Finer, "Abortion in the United States: Incidence and Access to Services, 2005," Guttmacher Institute, *Perspectives on Reproductive Health* 40, no. 1 (March 2008), www.guttmacher.org/pubs/journals/4000608.pdf.

14. "International Data Base World Population: 1950–2050," U.S. Census Bureau, July 9, 2015, http://www.census.gov/population/international/data/idb/worldpopgraph.php.

15. Goklany, *The Improving State of the World*, 47–49.

Kris Vallotton is the author of several books and is a much sought after international conference speaker. He has a passion to see people's lives transformed and to act as a catalyst for world transformation.

In 1998, Kris cofounded the Bethel School of Supernatural Ministry in Redding, California, which has grown to more than two thousand full-time students. Kris is the senior associate leader at Bethel Church and has been a part of Bill Johnson's apostolic team for more than three decades.

Kris is also the founder and CEO of Moral Revolution, an organization dedicated to a worldwide sexual reformation.

Kris and his wife, Kathy, have been happily married since 1975. They have four children and eight grandchildren.

You can contact Kris or find out more about him and his other ministry materials at www.krisvallotton.com, or you can download the KV Ministries app on your smartphone. You can also follow Kris and Kathy on Facebook (www.facebook.com/kvministries), Twitter (@kvministries) and Instagram (@kvministries).

More from Kris Vallotton

Curriculum Kits Available for Small Group and Church Use

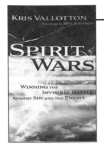

Through his personal story of demonic bondage and deliverance, Kris Vallotton reveals the diabolical lies and strategies of the enemy, showing you how to take hold of victory.

Spirit Wars

This essential guide for prophets reveals the foundational truths pivotal to prophetic ministry, providing you the critical advanced training you need to grow in your giftings.

School of the Prophets

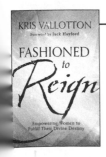

In this liberating teaching, Kris Vallotton shares God's true plan and purpose for women—in the Church and throughout creation. As daughters and sons of the King, it's time for us to work together to restore God's original design for biblical partnership.

Fashioned to Reign

✓Chosen

Stay up-to-date on your favorite books and authors with our free e-newsletters. Sign up today at chosenbooks.com.

Find us on Facebook. facebook.com/chosenbooks

Follow us on Twitter. @Chosen_Books

More from Kris Vallotton

While held captive on an Asian island, Tracy Evans cared for rebel guerillas. She sipped tea in a Mozambican hut while bullets whistled through the grass walls. She's inspired people like Kris Vallotton, Bill Johnson and Rolland and Heidi Baker. Now you, too, can meet this courageous woman—and discover what God can do through one person's raw faith and radical obedience.

Outrageous Courage (with Jason Vallotton)

In this intimate and honest book, Kris Vallotton addresses the root causes of purity issues, seeking to inspire a culture of love, honor and respect with people who walk in purity, passion and power. Our world needs a different kind of sexual revolution—one that transforms the way the world views sexuality, defines the unborn and embraces the family. Join the Moral Revolution!

Moral Revolution (with Jason Vallotton)

God uses difficult seasons and relationships to propel His children toward their destiny. Find out how to steward the hardest times of your life so that God can lay a foundation for complete restoration and empowerment for your future.

The Supernatural Power of Forgiveness (with Jason Vallotton)